# The Complete Guide to Cross-Platform Programming in Python

## Techniques, Frameworks, and Best Practices for Building Scalable Applications

THOMPSON CARTER

# Table of Contents

4

7

11

12

14

18

19

## INTRODUCTION

# *The Complete Guide to Cross-Platform Programming in Python*

The world of software development has changed dramatically over the past decade. With the rise of **cloud computing, mobile applications, and multi-platform accessibility**, developers are no longer confined to a single operating system or ecosystem. The demand for applications that run seamlessly across **Windows, macOS, Linux, mobile devices, and even the web** has never been higher.

This shift has made **cross-platform development** a crucial skill for modern programmers. And while many languages specialize in specific platforms, **Python** stands out as one of the most versatile, flexible, and powerful options for **developing cross-platform applications**.

This book, *The Complete Guide to Cross-Platform Programming in Python*, is designed to **empower developers** with the knowledge, tools, and best practices needed to build **scalable, performant, and secure applications** that work on multiple platforms.

# Why Python for Cross-Platform Development?

Python has consistently ranked as one of the **most popular programming languages** in the world, and for good reason. It offers:

22

- **A simple, readable syntax** that makes it easy to learn and use.
- **A vast ecosystem of libraries and frameworks** for everything from web development to machine learning.
- **Strong community support** with continuous improvements and updates.
- **Excellent cross-platform compatibility**, allowing code to run **on Windows, macOS, Linux, mobile, and even the web** with minimal changes.

# *Key Advantages of Python in Cross-Platform Development*

1. **Write Once, Run Anywhere** – With proper design patterns and tools, Python applications can run on **multiple operating systems** without significant modifications.
2. **Broad Framework Support** – Python provides powerful frameworks for **GUI, web, mobile, AI, and system automation**, ensuring developers have the right tools for any project.
3. **Integration with Other Technologies** – Python can work with **C, C++, Rust, WebAssembly, and cloud platforms**, making it highly extensible.
4. **Active Open-Source Community** – Thousands of developers contribute to Python's **ever-growing ecosystem**, ensuring **continuous improvements and long-term support**.

23

## What You Will Learn in This Book

This book is structured into **nine comprehensive parts**, guiding you through every aspect of **cross-platform programming in Python**.

# *Part 1: Foundations of Cross-Platform Programming*

- Understanding how **Python applications work across different operating systems**.
- Learning about **file system differences, platform APIs, and compatibility issues**.
- Setting up a **portable Python development environment**.

# *Part 2: Building Cross-Platform Graphical User Interfaces (GUI)*

- Exploring **Tkinter, PyQt, Kivy, and BeeWare** for desktop and mobile UI applications.
- Designing **modern user interfaces** that adapt to different screen sizes.
- Packaging GUI applications into **executable files** for Windows, macOS, and Linux.

# *Part 3: Developing Web-Based Cross-Platform Applications*

- Using **Flask, Django, and FastAPI** to create **scalable web applications**.

- Deploying Python apps **on cloud services (AWS, Google Cloud, Azure)**.
- Integrating **APIs, databases, and front-end technologies** for full-stack applications.

# Part 4: Cross-Platform Game and Mobile Development

- Using **Pygame, Godot, and Unity** for game development with Python.
- Building **mobile applications with Kivy and BeeWare** for Android and iOS.
- Optimizing **graphics, sound, and input handling** for different platforms.

# Part 5: Working with Databases Across Platforms

- Choosing the right database: **SQLite, PostgreSQL, MongoDB, and Firebase**.
- Using **SQLAlchemy and ORMs** for database abstraction.
- Deploying databases **on cloud platforms and edge devices**.

# Part 6: Automating and Scripting Across Platforms

- Writing **portable Python scripts** for **file management, system tasks, and network automation**.
- Using **subprocess, os, and Fabric** to execute platform-specific commands.

- Scheduling tasks with **Cron (Linux/macOS) and Task Scheduler (Windows)**.

# Part 7: Packaging and Distribution

- Creating **standalone executables with PyInstaller, cx_Freeze, and PyOxidizer**.
- Publishing applications on **PyPI, Snap, Homebrew, and App Stores**.
- Handling **dependencies, versioning, and updates** for cross-platform deployment.

# Part 8: Performance Optimization and Security

- Optimizing Python performance with **Cython, Numba, and PyPy**.
- Securing Python applications against **SQL injection, XSS, CSRF, and authentication attacks**.
- Encrypting and protecting **data storage, network communication, and user credentials**.

# Part 9: The Future of Cross-Platform Development

- Exploring **serverless computing** for scalable applications.
- Using **WebAssembly (Wasm) to run Python in the browser**.
- Integrating **Python with Rust** for high-performance cross-platform applications.
- Understanding **emerging trends in AI, automation, and cloud-based development**.

# Who Is This Book For?

This book is for **developers of all levels** who want to:

- Build **cross-platform Python applications** for **desktop, web, mobile, and IoT**.
- Learn how to **package, deploy, and scale Python applications** efficiently.
- Optimize Python code **for performance, security, and scalability**.
- Stay ahead of **emerging trends in cloud computing, WebAssembly, and AI**.

Whether you are a **beginner looking to explore cross-platform development** or an **experienced developer seeking to enhance your Python applications**, this book provides a **comprehensive guide** with **real-world examples, best practices, and industry insights**.

# Why This Book is Different

- **Real-World Examples** – Each chapter includes **practical projects and hands-on examples**.
- **Jargon-Free Explanations** – Complex topics are broken down into **easy-to-understand language**.
- **Future-Proof Knowledge** – Covers **cutting-edge technologies** like WebAssembly, AI, and serverless computing.
- **Cross-Platform Focus** – Learn how to make Python applications run **on any operating system or device**.

# How to Use This Book

- If you are new to **cross-platform development**, start with **Part 1** and work your way through each section.
- If you are interested in **a specific area (e.g., GUI, web, mobile, automation)**, jump directly to that section.
- Use the **code examples and best practices** to build and improve your own Python applications.
- Stay updated by **following Python's latest developments** and **experimenting with emerging technologies**.

# Final Thoughts

Cross-platform development is the **future of software engineering**, and Python is uniquely positioned to **bridge the gap between different platforms**. By mastering the techniques in this book, you will be able to **build scalable, efficient, and secure applications that work across multiple ecosystems**.

This book is not just about **writing code**—it's about **understanding the best practices, tools, and emerging trends** that will help you succeed in Python development for years to come.

So, whether you're building **desktop apps, mobile apps, web applications, or cloud services**, the journey to mastering **cross-platform Python development** starts here.

**Let's Get Started!**

# *Part 1*

# *Foundations of Cross-Platform Programming in Python*

# Chapter 1

# Introduction to Cross-Platform Development

Cross-platform programming is at the heart of modern software development. The ability to write code once and run it on multiple operating systems is essential for **software scalability, cost-efficiency, and user accessibility**. This chapter introduces the fundamental concepts of cross-platform development, explores why Python is a preferred language for this purpose, and discusses the challenges and benefits associated with cross-platform application development.

---

# What is Cross-Platform Programming?

Cross-platform programming refers to the practice of writing software that runs on multiple operating systems **without requiring significant modifications**. In traditional development, applications are often built separately for Windows, macOS, and Linux, leading to **increased development time, higher costs, and maintenance complexity**.

With cross-platform programming, a single codebase can be used across different environments, making development **more efficient, scalable, and accessible to a larger audience**.

Examples of cross-platform software include:

- **Web browsers like Google Chrome and Mozilla Firefox**, which run on multiple operating systems.
- **Productivity applications like Microsoft Office and LibreOffice**, available on Windows, macOS, and Linux.
- **Mobile apps using frameworks like Flutter and React Native**, allowing deployment on both Android and iOS.

Python, with its extensive libraries and platform-agnostic nature, is a powerful language for cross-platform development.

# Why Python is a Great Choice for Cross-Platform Development

Python is one of the most popular languages for cross-platform programming due to several reasons:

1. **Interpreted Language with Platform Independence**
   - Python does not require compilation into machine code, allowing the same script to run on different operating systems as long as Python is installed.
2. **Extensive Standard Library**
   - Python's built-in modules handle file operations, networking, threading, and database access in a way that abstracts OS-specific differences.
3. **Rich Ecosystem of Cross-Platform Frameworks**
   - Python provides various frameworks for different types of cross-platform applications:
     - **GUI applications:** Tkinter, PyQt, Kivy

- **Web applications:** Flask, Django, FastAPI
- **Mobile applications:** BeeWare, Kivy
- **Game development:** Pygame, Godot

4. **Strong Community Support and Documentation**
   o Python has an active developer community, making it easier to find resources, tools, and third-party libraries for cross-platform development.

5. **Compatibility with Other Languages**
   o Python can easily integrate with **C, C++, Java, and Rust**, making it versatile for cross-platform applications that require optimized performance.

6. **Automation and Scripting**
   o Python is widely used for cross-platform automation, such as **system administration, testing, and data processing**.

7. **Cloud and AI Integration**
   o Many cloud services and AI tools provide **Python SDKs** that enable seamless integration into cross-platform projects.

With these advantages, Python is widely used by developers building applications that need to function across different environments.

---

# *Challenges and Benefits of Cross-Platform Applications*

*Challenges of Cross-Platform Development*

While cross-platform programming offers flexibility, it also comes with challenges that developers must address:

1. **Performance Limitations**
   - Native applications (written specifically for one OS) often have better performance than cross-platform apps.
   - Some Python frameworks rely on **interpreters or virtual machines**, which may slow execution.

2. **UI/UX Inconsistencies**
   - Different operating systems have unique UI components and design guidelines.
   - A cross-platform application must **balance consistency with native OS aesthetics**.

3. **Device Compatibility Issues**
   - Hardware variations (different screen sizes, processors, and input methods) can create unexpected behavior.
   - Mobile applications need to account for **touchscreen interfaces, sensors, and performance constraints**.

4. **Dependency Management and OS-Specific Libraries**
   - Some Python modules work differently across platforms (e.g., file paths in Windows vs. Linux).
   - Developers need to test for **cross-platform compatibility** and manage dependencies carefully.

5. **Security and Permissions**
   - Different platforms have distinct **security policies, file permissions, and networking rules**.
   - Applications must comply with **each OS's security guidelines** to prevent vulnerabilities.

*Benefits of Cross-Platform Development*

Despite the challenges, cross-platform development offers **significant advantages**:

1. **Faster Development Time**

  - A single codebase reduces development effort compared to building separate applications for each platform.

2. **Lower Maintenance Costs**
   - Fixing bugs or adding features can be done once, rather than maintaining multiple codebases.

3. **Wider Market Reach**
   - A cross-platform application can **target users across different operating systems**, increasing adoption.

4. **Reusable Codebase**
   - Python libraries and modules can be reused across projects, enhancing **development efficiency**.

5. **Flexibility and Scalability**
   - Python-based applications can be easily **extended with plugins and integrated with emerging technologies**.

6. **Easier Updates and Deployment**
   - Cloud-based applications and web apps built with Python can be updated **without requiring users to install new versions**.

# *Conclusion*

Cross-platform development is essential for **modern software applications**, providing **flexibility, scalability, and cost-effectiveness**. Python is one of the best languages for this purpose due to its **platform independence, vast ecosystem, and ease of use**. However, developers must be aware of **performance trade-offs, UI consistency challenges, and security considerations**.

In the next chapter, we will explore **how to set up the Python environment for cross-platform development**, including **dependency management, virtualization, and using tools like Docker for consistency across platforms**.

# *What's Next?*

In **Chapter 2**, we will cover:

- Installing and managing Python versions for different operating systems
- Setting up virtual environments and handling dependencies
- Using Docker for cross-platform compatibility

By understanding **how to configure Python for multi-platform projects**, developers can **avoid compatibility issues and build scalable applications with confidence**.

This chapter provides **a clear, structured introduction to cross-platform development with Python**, balancing **technical concepts with real-world examples**. Let me know if you'd like any refinements before moving to **Chapter 2: Setting Up Your Python Environment!**

# Chapter 2

# Setting Up Your Python Environment

Cross-platform development requires a **consistent and well-configured Python environment** to ensure that applications run **seamlessly across multiple operating systems**. Choosing the **right Python version, managing dependencies properly, and using containerization** can prevent compatibility issues and streamline development.

This chapter explores:

1. Choosing the right Python version
2. Managing dependencies with `pip` and virtual environments
3. Using Docker and containerization for cross-platform consistency

---

# Choosing the Right Python Version

Python has multiple active versions, and choosing the right one is **crucial for compatibility and performance**. While newer versions offer **performance improvements and new features**, some libraries may not yet support them.

*Which Python Version Should You Use?*

- **Python 3.x:** Python 2 has been deprecated since **January 1, 2020**, making **Python 3.x the standard for modern development**.

- **Long-Term Support (LTS) Versions:** It is recommended to use **the latest stable Python release** (e.g., **Python 3.11 or later**) to ensure security and performance.
- **Matching the Target Platform:**
  - If deploying on **legacy systems**, ensure that the **chosen Python version is compatible** with the OS.
  - For **web applications**, verify **hosting service compatibility** (e.g., some cloud platforms may not support the latest Python versions immediately).

*Installing Python on Different Platforms*

- **Windows**
  - Download the latest Python installer from **python.org**.
  - Enable the **"Add Python to PATH"** option during installation to use Python from the command line.
- **macOS**
  - Python 3 is pre-installed on macOS, but it is best to install the latest version using **Homebrew**:

```
nginx

brew install python
```

- **Linux**
  - Most Linux distributions come with Python pre-installed. Update it using the package manager:

```
sql

sudo apt update && sudo apt install python3
```

- **Cross-Version Management**

37

○ Use **pyenv** to switch between Python versions easily:

```csharp
pyenv install 3.11.2
pyenv global 3.11.2
```

Choosing the right Python version ensures that your application remains **stable, secure, and compatible across multiple environments**.

# Managing Dependencies with pip and Virtual Environments

A major challenge in cross-platform development is **handling dependencies**. Different platforms may have different versions of libraries, leading to compatibility issues. Using **virtual environments** allows developers to isolate dependencies for each project.

*1. Using pip to Manage Packages*

Python's **pip (Python Package Installer)** is used to install and manage external libraries.

• **Installing a package:**

```nginx
pip install requests
```

• **Listing installed packages:**

```
nginx

pip list
```

- **Freezing dependencies (for easy replication across platforms):**

```
pgsql

pip freeze > requirements.txt
```

- **Installing dependencies from a file:**

```
nginx

pip install -r requirements.txt
```

*2. Creating and Using Virtual Environments*

Virtual environments **prevent dependency conflicts** by keeping each project's dependencies separate.

- **Creating a virtual environment:**

```
nginx

python -m venv my_project_env
```

- **Activating the environment:**
  - ○ Windows:

```
my_project_env\Scripts\activate
```

  - ○ macOS/Linux:

```
bash

source my_project_env/bin/activate
```

39

- **Deactivating the environment:**

```
nginx

deactivate
```

Using virtual environments ensures that **dependencies are isolated**, making projects more **portable and reproducible across platforms**.

---

# *Using Docker and Containerization for Consistency*

While virtual environments help manage dependencies, **Docker provides an even more robust solution** by creating a **standardized runtime environment** across different operating systems.

*1. What is Docker?*

Docker allows applications to run in **lightweight, portable containers**, ensuring that they behave the same across different machines.

- **Why use Docker for cross-platform development?**
  - Eliminates **"works on my machine"** issues.
  - Packages **all dependencies, libraries, and runtime environments** into a container.
  - Enables **easy deployment across Windows, macOS, and Linux**.

40

*2. Installing Docker*

- **Windows/macOS:** Download and install **Docker Desktop** from **docker.com**.
- **Linux:** Install using the package manager:

```lua
sudo apt install docker.io
```

- Verify installation:

```css
docker --version
```

*3. Creating a Dockerized Python Environment*

A **Dockerfile** defines the environment for your Python application.

- **Example Dockerfile:**

```bash
FROM python:3.11
WORKDIR /app
COPY . /app
RUN pip install -r requirements.txt
CMD ["python", "app.py"]
```

- **Building the Docker image:**

```perl
docker build -t my-python-app .
```

- **Running the container:**

```arduino
```

41

```
docker run -p 5000:5000 my-python-app
```

*4. Using Docker Compose for Multi-Container Applications*

For applications that need **databases, APIs, or additional services**, Docker Compose simplifies setup.

- **Example `docker-compose.yml` for a Flask app with PostgreSQL:**

```yaml
yaml

version: '3'
services:
  web:
    build: .
    ports:
      - "5000:5000"
    depends_on:
      - db
  db:
    image: postgres:latest
    environment:
      POSTGRES_USER: user
      POSTGRES_PASSWORD: password
```

- **Starting the application:**

```
docker-compose up
```

Using Docker ensures that **Python applications run consistently across different platforms**, making it easier to **deploy, test, and scale projects**.

# *Conclusion*

42

A well-configured Python environment is essential for **smooth cross-platform development**. By choosing the **right Python version, managing dependencies with pip and virtual environments, and leveraging Docker for containerization**, developers can **eliminate compatibility issues and build scalable applications efficiently**.

# *Key Takeaways*

- Choosing the latest **LTS Python version** improves **security and stability**.
- Using **pip and virtual environments** isolates dependencies, preventing conflicts.
- Docker **creates a uniform development environment** that runs consistently across platforms.

---

# *What's Next?*

In **Chapter 3**, we will explore:

- Understanding **OS-level differences in file systems, permissions, and system calls**.
- Adapting Python applications to handle **cross-platform challenges**.
- Best practices for **writing platform-independent Python code**.

With **a properly set up Python environment**, developers are now ready to **tackle platform-specific challenges** and build truly **portable applications**.

# *Final Notes*

This chapter **provides a structured, in-depth approach** to setting up a Python environment for **cross-platform development**, balancing **technical explanations with real-world applications**. Let me know if you'd like any refinements before moving to **Chapter 3: Understanding Platform Differences**!

# Chapter 3

# Understanding Platform Differences

Cross-platform programming requires a deep understanding of **how different operating systems handle file systems, APIs, and system interactions**. Python provides tools to manage these differences, but developers must be aware of OS-specific behavior to ensure that applications run smoothly across **Windows, macOS, Linux, Android, and iOS**.

This chapter explores:

1. OS-level differences in Windows, macOS, Linux, Android, and iOS
2. File system variations and handling paths correctly
3. Managing platform-specific APIs in a cross-platform Python application

---

# OS-Level Differences (Windows, macOS, Linux, Android, iOS)

Operating systems have **fundamental differences** in how they handle **system resources, file paths, permissions, and background processes**. Python provides the `os` and `platform` modules to detect and adapt to these variations.

## 1. Windows vs. macOS vs. Linux

| Feature | Windows | macOS | Linux |
|---|---|---|---|
| File Path Separator | Backslash (\) | Forward slash (/) | Forward slash (/) |
| Case Sensitivity | Case-insensitive (`file.txt` = `File.txt`) | Case-sensitive (`file.txt` ≠ `File.txt`) | Case-sensitive (`file.txt` ≠ `File.txt`) |
| Executable Files | `.exe, .bat` | Unix executables (`.sh`) | Unix executables (`.sh`) |
| Line Endings | `\r\n` (CRLF) | `\n` (LF) | `\n` (LF) |
| Default Shell | `cmd.exe`, PowerShell | `zsh, bash` | `bash, sh` |
| User Home Directory | `C:\Users\usern ame` | `/Users/usern ame` | `/home/usern ame` |
| Permissions Model | User Account Control (UAC) | Unix-style permissions (`chmod`) | Unix-style permissions (`chmod`) |

- **Windows uses backslashes (\) in file paths**, while macOS and Linux use forward slashes (/).
- **Linux and macOS are case-sensitive**, whereas Windows is not.
- **Windows uses different line endings (\r\n)**, which can cause issues when handling text files across platforms.

46

*2. Android and iOS Considerations*

Python is **not natively supported on mobile operating systems**, but frameworks like **Kivy and BeeWare** enable Python applications to run on Android and iOS.

- **Android uses a Linux-based kernel**, so it shares many similarities with Linux.
- **iOS has stricter security policies**, restricting background processes and requiring apps to be packaged as `.ipa` files.
- **Both platforms use sandboxing**, meaning applications have limited access to system files.

To detect the platform in Python, use the `platform` module:

```python
import platform

print(platform.system())     # Output: Windows, Linux, Darwin (macOS)
print(platform.release())   # Output: OS version
print(platform.machine())         #      Output: Architecture (x86_64, ARM)
```

# *File System Variations*

Handling files and directories across platforms requires **careful management of paths, encodings, and file permissions**.

*1. Working with File Paths in a Cross-Platform Way*

Instead of hardcoding file paths, use Python's `os.path` or `pathlib` for platform-independent path handling.

47

```python
python

import os

# Cross-platform way to join file paths
file_path    =    os.path.join("home",    "user",
"documents", "file.txt")
print(file_path)              #        Windows:
home\user\documents\file.txt    |    Linux/macOS:
home/user/documents/file.txt
```

With `pathlib` (recommended for Python 3.6+):

```python
python

from pathlib import Path

file_path   =   Path.home()   /   "documents"   /
"file.txt"
print(file_path)  # Automatically adapts to the
OS
```

*2. Handling Line Endings Correctly*

To avoid issues with line endings (\n vs \r\n), open files in **universal newline mode**:

```python
python

with open("file.txt", "r", newline='') as file:
    content = file.read()
```

*3. File Permissions and Execution*

On Linux/macOS, files require **execution permissions (chmod)**:

```bash
bash

chmod +x script.py
```

To check and modify file permissions in Python:

```python
python

import os
import stat

file_path = "script.py"

# Check if file is executable
if os.access(file_path, os.X_OK):
    print("File is executable")

# Make file executable
os.chmod(file_path, os.stat(file_path).st_mode |
stat.S_IXUSR)
```

# *Managing Platform-Specific APIs*

Some system operations, like **accessing system info, executing commands, or handling OS-specific features**, require platform-aware coding.

*1. Running System Commands*

Use `subprocess` instead of `os.system()` for **better security and cross-platform compatibility**.

```python
python

import subprocess

# Windows command
if platform.system() == "Windows":
    result = subprocess.run(["dir"], shell=True,
capture_output=True, text=True)

# macOS/Linux command
else:
    result = subprocess.run(["ls",    "-la"],
capture_output=True, text=True)
```

49

```
print(result.stdout)
```
*2. Detecting and Using Platform-Specific Features*

Sometimes, platform-specific libraries are needed. The best practice is to **conditionally import modules**:

```python
import platform

if platform.system() == "Windows":
    import ctypes  # Windows-specific module
    ctypes.windll.user32.MessageBoxW(0,  "Hello, Windows!", "Message", 1)

elif platform.system() == "Darwin":  # macOS
    import subprocess
    subprocess.run(["osascript", "-e", 'display dialog "Hello, macOS!"'])

else:  # Linux
    print("Hello, Linux!")
```
*3. Using shutil for Cross-Platform File Operations*

The shutil module provides a **portable way** to move, copy, and delete files:

```python
import shutil

# Copying a file (works across platforms)
shutil.copy("source.txt", "destination.txt")

# Moving a file
shutil.move("source.txt",
"new_folder/source.txt")

# Deleting a file
shutil.rmtree("old_folder")
```

# *Conclusion*

Cross-platform development requires **understanding OS-level differences** to ensure that Python applications run smoothly on **Windows, macOS, Linux, Android, and iOS**. By using **platform-aware programming techniques**, developers can avoid common pitfalls related to **file paths, system commands, and OS-specific dependencies**.

## *Key Takeaways*

- Use **Python's `platform` module** to detect the operating system dynamically.
- Handle **file paths and line endings correctly** with `os.path` or `pathlib`.
- Manage **file permissions** carefully, especially on Linux/macOS.
- Use **subprocess** instead of `os.system()` for better cross-platform command execution.
- Avoid **hardcoded OS-specific code**, and use conditional imports when necessary.

## *What's Next?*

In **Chapter 4**, we will cover:

- Writing **platform-independent code** that avoids OS-specific issues
- Strategies for **modularizing and organizing code** for portability

- Best practices for **debugging and testing across multiple platforms**

Understanding **platform differences** is a fundamental step toward building **robust, scalable, and truly cross-platform applications in Python**.

---

This chapter **explains platform-specific challenges clearly, with real-world code examples**. Let me know if you'd like any refinements before moving to **Chapter 4: Code Portability and Writing Platform-Agnostic Code**!

# Chapter 4

# *Code Portability and Writing Platform-Agnostic Code*

Cross-platform development in Python requires writing **OS-independent code** that works seamlessly on **Windows, macOS, Linux, and even mobile platforms like Android and iOS**. Code portability ensures that applications remain **consistent, stable, and easy to maintain** across different environments.

This chapter explores:

1. Best practices for writing OS-independent Python code
2. Handling line endings, encoding, and system paths correctly
3. Using the `os` and `sys` modules effectively for cross-platform compatibility

---

# *Best Practices for Writing OS-Independent Python Code*

Writing **platform-agnostic** code means avoiding **hardcoded OS-specific logic** and using Python's **built-in tools to handle system differences dynamically**.

*1. Use* `platform` *and* `sys` *to Detect the Operating System*

Python provides the `platform` module to check which OS the script is running on.

```python

import platform

system_name = platform.system()

if system_name == "Windows":
    print("Running on Windows")
elif system_name == "Darwin":   # macOS
    print("Running on macOS")
elif system_name == "Linux":
    print("Running on Linux")
else:
    print("Unknown OS")
```

This approach allows **conditional execution of OS-specific logic** while maintaining a **single codebase**.

---

*2. Avoid Hardcoded File Paths and Use* `pathlib` *for Path Handling*

File paths differ across operating systems:

- **Windows uses backslashes (\)**
- **Linux/macOS use forward slashes (/)**
- **Some platforms have different home directory structures**

Using Python's `pathlib` ensures portability:

```python

from pathlib import Path
```

```
# Get the user's home directory in a cross-
platform way
home_dir = Path.home()
print(home_dir)  # Windows: C:\Users\username |
Linux/macOS: /home/username

# Create a platform-independent file path
file_path = home_dir / "documents" / "myfile.txt"
print(file_path)              #        Windows:
C:\Users\username\documents\myfile.txt
                 #                    Linux/macOS:
/home/username/documents/myfile.txt
```

*3. Use `shutil` for File Operations Instead of OS-Specific Commands*

Instead of using `os.system("copy file.txt newfile.txt")` (Windows) or `os.system("cp file.txt newfile.txt")` (Linux/macOS), use `shutil` for **cross-platform file copying**:

```
python

import shutil

# Copy a file (works across all platforms)
shutil.copy("source.txt", "destination.txt")

# Move a file
shutil.move("source.txt",
"new_folder/source.txt")

# Delete a folder
shutil.rmtree("old_folder")
```

*4. Use* `tempfile` *for Temporary Files*

Some OS-specific **temporary file locations** may cause errors if accessed incorrectly. Python's `tempfile` module automatically creates temp files **compatible across all platforms**:

python

```
import tempfile

with tempfile.NamedTemporaryFile(delete=False)
as temp_file:
    temp_file.write(b"Temporary data")
    print("Temporary        file        path:",
temp_file.name)
```

# *Handling Line Endings, Encoding, and System Paths*

*1. Line Endings (*`\r\n`*vs.*`\n`*)*

Different operating systems handle text line endings differently:

- **Windows uses `\r\n` (Carriage Return + Line Feed)**
- **Linux/macOS use `\n` (Line Feed only)**

To ensure consistent line endings when reading/writing files, use Python's **universal newline mode (`newline=''`)**:

python

```
# Open file in universal newline mode (preserves
platform compatibility)
```

56

```
with open("example.txt", "r", newline='') as
file:
    content = file.readlines()
```

Alternatively, normalize line endings in Python:

```python
# Convert Windows line endings (\r\n) to
Linux/macOS (\n)
with open("example.txt", "r") as file:
    content = file.read().replace("\r\n", "\n")
```

## 2. Handling Character Encodings

Different operating systems may use different **default text encodings**, leading to errors when reading non-ASCII files.

To **ensure cross-platform compatibility**, explicitly specify **UTF-8 encoding** when handling text files:

```python
# Always specify encoding to avoid compatibility
issues
with open("example.txt", "r", encoding="utf-8")
as file:
    content = file.read()
```

If encoding issues arise, use `chardet` to **detect the file encoding**:

```python
import chardet

with open("example.txt", "rb") as file:
    raw_data = file.read()

encoding_info = chardet.detect(raw_data)
```

```
print("Detected                              encoding:",
encoding_info["encoding"])
```

---

### 3. Using os.path for File and Directory Operations

Python's os.path module provides **portable file handling methods**.

python

```
import os

# Get the absolute path of a file
abs_path = os.path.abspath("file.txt")
print(abs_path)

# Get the directory of the current script
script_dir                                      =
os.path.dirname(os.path.abspath(__file__))
print(script_dir)

# Check if a file exists
if os.path.exists("file.txt"):
    print("File exists")
```

For **cross-platform path joining**, use os.path.join():

python

```
# Avoid hardcoding file paths
file_path = os.path.join("folder", "subfolder",
"file.txt")
print(file_path)                    #       Windows:
folder\subfolder\file.txt      |      Linux/macOS:
folder/subfolder/file.txt
```

---

# *Using the os and sys Modules Effectively*

Python's `os` and `sys` modules provide **platform-aware methods** for interacting with the operating system.

*1. Detecting the OS Type with `os.name` and `platform.system()`*

```python
import os

if os.name == "nt":  # Windows
    print("Running on Windows")
elif os.name == "posix":  # Linux/macOS
    print("Running on Unix-based OS")
```

*2. Executing OS Commands with `subprocess` Instead of `os.system()`*

Instead of using `os.system()`, use `subprocess` for **better security and compatibility**:

```python
import subprocess

# Windows command
if os.name == "nt":
    result = subprocess.run(["dir"], shell=True, capture_output=True, text=True)

# macOS/Linux command
else:
    result = subprocess.run(["ls", "-la"], capture_output=True, text=True)

print(result.stdout)
```

*3. Handling Command-Line Arguments with `sys.argv`*

Use `sys.argv` to **accept user input from the command line** across all platforms:

```python
import sys

if len(sys.argv) > 1:
    print("Argument received:", sys.argv[1])
else:
    print("No argument provided")
```

Run the script from the command line:

```bash
python script.py HelloWorld
```

Output:

```yaml
Argument received: HelloWorld
```

# *Conclusion*

Writing **platform-agnostic Python code** is essential for **cross-platform compatibility**. By following best practices for **file handling, encoding, and OS-level interactions**, developers can build applications that work seamlessly across **Windows, macOS, Linux, and mobile devices**.

60

# *Key Takeaways*

- Use `platform` **and** `sys` to detect the OS and adapt accordingly.
- Avoid hardcoded file paths—use `pathlib` and `os.path` for portability.
- Handle text files with **universal line endings** (`newline=' '`) and explicit encoding (`utf-8`).
- Use **subprocess** instead of `os.system()` for executing OS commands securely.

# *What's Next?*

In **Chapter 5**, we will explore:

- Python's **standard library tools for cross-platform development**
- How `platform`, `shutil`, and `pathlib` simplify cross-platform coding
- Practical examples of **multi-platform file operations and system interactions**

By mastering **OS-independent programming techniques**, developers can **write truly portable Python applications**.

This chapter provides **real-world examples and clear explanations** to help developers write **cross-platform Python code efficiently**. Let me know if you'd like any refinements before moving to **Chapter 5: Python Standard Library for Cross-Platform Development!**

# Chapter 5

# Python Standard Library for Cross-Platform Development

The **Python Standard Library** includes powerful modules that enable **cross-platform development without requiring third-party dependencies**. By leveraging built-in tools such as `platform, shutil, subprocess, and pathlib`, developers can **write adaptable and portable code** that runs seamlessly across **Windows, macOS, Linux, and even mobile platforms**.

This chapter explores:

1. Overview of built-in modules that simplify cross-platform work
2. Using `platform, shutil, subprocess, and pathlib`
3. Detecting system properties and adapting dynamically

---

# Overview of Built-in Modules That Simplify Cross-Platform Work

Python provides a robust **standard library** with modules that help manage **OS-specific behavior, file operations, and system interactions** without requiring additional dependencies.

*1. Key Modules for Cross-Platform Development*

- `platform` – Detects the operating system and hardware properties.
- `os` – Interacts with the operating system (file paths, environment variables).
- `shutil` – Performs high-level file operations (copy, move, delete).
- `subprocess` – Executes system commands in a platform-independent manner.
- `pathlib` – Handles file paths and directories in an OS-agnostic way.

Using these modules ensures that **Python applications behave consistently across multiple platforms** without requiring custom platform-specific code.

# *Using `platform` to Detect System Properties*

The `platform` module provides information about the **operating system, processor, and system version**, allowing applications to **adapt dynamically**.

*1. Detecting the Operating System*

```python

import platform

os_name = platform.system()

if os_name == "Windows":
    print("Running on Windows")
elif os_name == "Darwin":  # macOS
```

63

```
    print("Running on macOS")
elif os_name == "Linux":
    print("Running on Linux")
else:
    print("Unknown OS")
```

*2. Getting System Information*

python

```
print("OS:", platform.system())    # Windows,
Linux, Darwin (macOS)
print("OS Version:", platform.version())
print("OS Release:", platform.release())
print("Architecture:",
platform.architecture()[0])  # 64-bit or 32-bit
print("Processor:", platform.processor())
print("Machine:", platform.machine())  # x86_64,
ARM, etc.
```

This information can be used to **customize application behavior** based on the system's capabilities.

---

# *Using* `shutil` *for Cross-Platform File Operations*

The `shutil` module provides **high-level file and directory operations**, ensuring that **file handling works consistently across different operating systems**.

*1. Copying and Moving Files*

python

```
import shutil

# Copy a file
shutil.copy("source.txt", "destination.txt")
```

64

```
# Move a file
shutil.move("source.txt",
"new_location/source.txt")
```

*2. Deleting Files and Directories*
```
python

import shutil

# Remove a directory and all its contents
shutil.rmtree("old_folder")
```

Using `shutil` ensures that **file operations work on Windows, macOS, and Linux without OS-specific commands**.

---

# *Using subprocess for System Commands*

Instead of using **OS-dependent system commands**, the `subprocess` module allows **secure and cross-platform execution of commands**.

*1. Running System Commands in a Platform-Independent Way*
```
python

import subprocess

# Windows command
if platform.system() == "Windows":
    result = subprocess.run(["dir"], shell=True,
capture_output=True, text=True)

# macOS/Linux command
else:
    result  =  subprocess.run(["ls",  "-la"],
capture_output=True, text=True)

print(result.stdout)
```

*2. Running External Programs*
python

```
import subprocess

# Open a text file with the default system
application
subprocess.run(["notepad",    "file.txt"]    if
platform.system()  ==  "Windows"  else  ["open",
"file.txt"])
```

Using subprocess **improves security and ensures compatibility** across different platforms.

---

# *Using* `pathlib` *for Cross-Platform Path Handling*

File paths differ between operating systems:

- **Windows uses backslashes (\)**
- **Linux/macOS use forward slashes (/)**
- **Some platforms have different directory structures (e.g., user home directories)**

*1. Creating Platform-Independent Paths*
python

```
from pathlib import Path

# Get the user's home directory
home_dir = Path.home()
print(home_dir)  # Windows: C:\Users\username |
Linux/macOS: /home/username

# Create a cross-platform file path
file_path = home_dir / "documents" / "myfile.txt"
```

```
print(file_path)                    #       Windows:
C:\Users\username\documents\myfile.txt
                  #                  Linux/macOS:
/home/username/documents/myfile.txt
```

*2. Checking File Existence and Modifying Paths*
```
python
```

```python
from pathlib import Path

file_path = Path("data.txt")

# Check if file exists
if file_path.exists():
    print("File exists")

# Get absolute path
print(file_path.resolve())
```

Using `pathlib` ensures that file paths **work correctly across all operating systems**.

---

# *Detecting System Properties and Adapting Dynamically*

*1. Checking Available Processors*
```
python
```

```python
import os

# Get the number of CPU cores
cpu_count = os.cpu_count()
print(f"Available CPU cores: {cpu_count}")
```
*2. Handling Environment Variables Cross-Platform*

Environment variables store **system configurations**, which may differ between OS environments.

67

```python
python

import os

# Get environment variable
home_dir      =      os.getenv("HOME")      if
platform.system()      !=      "Windows"      else
os.getenv("USERPROFILE")
print("User Home Directory:", home_dir)
```

*3. Using Temporary Files for Cross-Platform Compatibility*

```python
python

import tempfile

# Create a temporary file
with     tempfile.NamedTemporaryFile(delete=False)
as temp_file:
    temp_file.write(b"Temporary data")
    print("Temporary      file      path:",
temp_file.name)
```

These methods ensure **dynamic adaptability** across different system environments.

---

# *Conclusion*

By using **Python's built-in modules**, developers can write **cross-platform applications without relying on third-party dependencies**. Modules like `platform`, `shutil`, `subprocess`, and `pathlib` make it easier to **detect system properties, handle files, and execute system commands in a portable way**.

# *Key Takeaways*

- Use `platform` to **detect the OS and hardware** dynamically.
- Use `shutil` instead of OS-specific commands for **copying, moving, and deleting files**.
- Use `subprocess` for executing system commands **safely and cross-platform**.
- Use `pathlib` for **path management to avoid OS-specific path issues**.
- Manage **system properties dynamically** with `os` and environment variables.

# *What's Next?*

In **Chapter 6**, we will explore:

- Choosing the **right GUI framework** for cross-platform applications.
- Comparing **Tkinter, PyQt, Kivy, and wxPython** for GUI development.
- Best practices for **building graphical applications that work on Windows, macOS, and Linux**.

With a **strong foundation in Python's standard library**, developers can now move forward with **building cross-platform applications that require user interfaces and graphical elements**.

This chapter **provides practical insights and real-world code examples** to help developers write **cross-platform**

**Python applications efficiently**. Let me know if you'd like any refinements before moving to **Chapter 6: Choosing the Right GUI Framework**!

# Chapter 6

# *Choosing the Right GUI Framework*

Graphical User Interface (GUI) applications are an essential part of software development, enabling users to interact visually with programs. Python offers multiple **cross-platform GUI frameworks**, each with its own strengths and weaknesses. Choosing the **right framework** depends on factors like **performance, scalability, mobile support, and ease of development**.

This chapter explores:

1. A **comparison of Tkinter, PyQt, Kivy, PySide, wxPython, and Flutter**
2. The **pros and cons of each framework**
3. **Selecting a framework** based on project requirements

# *Comparison of Python GUI Frameworks*

Python supports **multiple cross-platform GUI frameworks** that work on **Windows, macOS, and Linux**. Some also extend support to **mobile platforms like Android and iOS**.

## 1. Overview of GUI Frameworks

| Framework | Platforms | Mobile Support | Ease of Use | Performance | Best Use Cases |
|---|---|---|---|---|---|
| Tkinter | Windows, macOS, Linux | No | Simple | Low | Small desktop apps, built-in Python GUI |
| PyQt | Windows, macOS, Linux | No | Moderate | High | Feature-rich applications, enterprise software |
| PySide | Windows, macOS, Linux | No | Moderate | High | Alternative to PyQt (same Qt backend) |
| wxPython | Windows, macOS, Linux | No | Moderate | High | Native-looking desktop applications |
| Kivy | Windows, macOS, Linux, Android, iOS | Yes | Moderate | Medium | Mobile & touch-based applications |

| Framework | Platforms | Mobile Support | Ease of Use | Performance | Best Use Cases |
|---|---|---|---|---|---|
| Flutter (with PyFlutter) | Windows, macOS, Linux, Android, iOS | Yes | Hard | High | Cross-platform mobile & desktop applications |

Each framework is designed for **specific use cases**, making it essential to choose the **right one based on your project's needs**.

# Pros and Cons of Each Framework

*1. Tkinter: The Built-in Standard*

Tkinter is **Python's default GUI framework**, making it easy to learn and use.

**Pros:**

- Built into Python (no extra installation required)
- Lightweight and simple to use
- Works on Windows, macOS, and Linux
- Good for small GUI applications

**Cons:**

- Outdated look and feel

73

- Lacks advanced widgets and customization
- Not suitable for modern, complex applications

**Best for:** Small desktop utilities, beginner projects.

---

*2. PyQt: The Powerful and Feature-Rich Choice*

PyQt is based on **Qt**, a **highly customizable** GUI toolkit used in professional applications.

**Pros:**

- Modern and feature-rich UI components
- High performance
- Supports multi-threading and complex applications
- Large developer community

**Cons:**

- **Commercial license required** for closed-source applications
- More complex than Tkinter
- Steeper learning curve

**Best for:** Large-scale desktop applications, enterprise software.

---

*3. PySide: The Open-Source Alternative to PyQt*

PySide also uses the Qt framework but is **fully open-source**.

**Pros:**

- Open-source and free for commercial use
- Similar to PyQt, making it easy to switch
- Good for building modern, cross-platform apps

## Cons:

- **Less community support** compared to PyQt
- Slightly **less mature documentation**

**Best for:** Open-source projects that require PyQt-like features.

---

*4. wxPython: The Native Look and Feel*

wxPython provides **native UI components**, making applications **look like they belong to the OS**.

## Pros:

- Uses native OS widgets for a familiar look
- Faster than Tkinter
- Good documentation and active community

## Cons:

- Can be more **complex** than Tkinter
- Not as feature-rich as Qt-based frameworks

**Best for:** Applications where **native look-and-feel is critical**.

---

*5. Kivy: The Best Choice for Mobile and Touch-Based Apps*

Kivy is designed for **multi-touch and mobile applications**, supporting **Android and iOS**.

## Pros:

- Works on **Windows, macOS, Linux, Android, and iOS**
- Supports touch and gesture-based UIs
- Good for dynamic and interactive apps
- Open-source

## Cons:

- Not ideal for **traditional desktop applications**
- UI style is **not native-looking**
- **Learning curve for Kivy language (kv)**

**Best for:** Mobile applications, games, and touch-based software.

---

*6. Flutter (PyFlutter): The Modern Cross-Platform Mobile Choice*

Flutter, originally built for **Dart**, is now usable with Python through **PyFlutter**, allowing the creation of **fully cross-platform mobile and desktop apps**.

## Pros:

- Works on **Windows, macOS, Linux, Android, and iOS**
- High performance, **native-like UI**
- Large ecosystem and support from Google

## Cons:

- **More complex setup**
- Requires knowledge of **Flutter's UI paradigm**
- Smaller Python community support

**Best for: Full-fledged mobile applications with modern UI.**

# *Selecting a Framework Based on Project Requirements*

Choosing the **right GUI framework** depends on factors like **target platforms, complexity, and performance needs**.

*1. For Simple Desktop Applications*

- **Best choice:** Tkinter
- **Example use cases:** File organizers, text editors, calculator apps

*2. For Enterprise-Grade Desktop Applications*

- **Best choice:** PyQt or PySide
- **Example use cases:** Financial software, data analysis tools

*3. For Native-Looking Applications*

- **Best choice:** wxPython
- **Example use cases:** System utilities, configuration tools

*4. For Mobile and Touch-Based Applications*

- **Best choice:** Kivy or Flutter (PyFlutter)
- **Example use cases:** Mobile games, touchscreen kiosks

*5. For Full Cross-Platform Desktop and Mobile*

- **Best choice:** Flutter (PyFlutter)
- **Example use cases:** Business apps, productivity tools

---

# *Conclusion*

Choosing the **right GUI framework** depends on **project requirements, platform targets, and UI needs**.

# *Key Takeaways*

- **Tkinter** is best for **small desktop applications**.
- **PyQt/PySide** are ideal for **enterprise applications**.
- **wxPython** provides a **native look-and-feel**.
- **Kivy** is great for **mobile and multi-touch applications**.
- **Flutter (PyFlutter)** offers **high-performance cross-platform solutions**.

---

# *What's Next?*

In **Chapter 7**, we will:

- Learn how to **build a cross-platform GUI application using Tkinter**.

- Explore **basic UI elements, events, and packaging for Windows, macOS, and Linux**.
- Develop a **simple Python GUI program that runs on multiple platforms**.

By understanding **the strengths and weaknesses of each GUI framework**, developers can **make informed decisions** about **which tool best suits their project needs**.

This chapter provides **a clear comparison of Python's GUI frameworks**, ensuring that developers can **select the best option for their project**

# Chapter 7

# Building Cross-Platform Applications with Tkinter

Tkinter is Python's **default GUI toolkit**, making it an excellent choice for **simple, cross-platform applications**. Since it is included with Python, Tkinter allows developers to **build graphical applications without installing additional libraries**.

This chapter explores:

1. Introduction to Tkinter and its advantages
2. Designing basic UI components (**buttons, labels, menus**)
3. Packaging a Tkinter application for **Windows, macOS, and Linux**

## Introduction to Tkinter

Tkinter is **lightweight, easy to use, and works across all major operating systems**. It is built on **Tcl/Tk**, a GUI toolkit that provides basic UI components like **buttons, text fields, and menus**.

# Why Use Tkinter?

- **Included with Python** – No additional installation required.
- **Cross-platform** – Works on **Windows, macOS, and Linux**.

- **Easy to learn** – Ideal for beginners and simple GUI applications.
- **Fast development** – Build and prototype applications quickly.

# *Limitations of Tkinter*

- **Limited styling options** – UIs may look outdated compared to modern frameworks like PyQt or Kivy.
- **Not ideal for complex applications** – Lacks advanced features needed for professional-grade software.
- **Minimal mobile support** – Does not work on Android or iOS.

Despite these limitations, **Tkinter remains a great choice** for **small-scale, lightweight GUI applications**.

# Designing Basic UI Components with Tkinter

## *Setting Up a Basic Tkinter Window*

Every Tkinter application starts by **creating a root window** using tk.Tk().

```python

import tkinter as tk

# Create the main window
root = tk.Tk()
root.title("Cross-Platform Tkinter App")
root.geometry("400x300")  # Set window size
```

81

```
# Run the application loop
root.mainloop()
```

This code creates a **simple empty window** with a title and a defined size. The `mainloop()` method **keeps the window open**, waiting for user interaction.

# *Adding Labels, Buttons, and Entry Fields*

UI components in Tkinter are called **widgets**. Some common widgets include:

- **Labels (`Label`)** – Display text.
- **Buttons (`Button`)** – Trigger actions.
- **Text Entry (`Entry`)** – Allow user input.

```python
python

import tkinter as tk

# Create main window
root = tk.Tk()
root.title("Basic UI Components")

# Create a label
label = tk.Label(root, text="Hello, Tkinter!",
font=("Arial", 14))
label.pack(pady=10)

# Create an entry field
entry = tk.Entry(root, width=30)
entry.pack(pady=5)

# Define a button action
```

```
def on_button_click():
    user_text = entry.get()
    label.config(text=f"You              entered:
{user_text}")

# Create a button
button    =    tk.Button(root,    text="Submit",
command=on_button_click)
button.pack(pady=10)

# Run the application
root.mainloop()
```

# *Explanation*

- **Label()** displays static text.
- **Entry()** allows user input.
- **Button()** triggers an action (on_button_click).
- **pack()** arranges widgets in the window.

This example creates a **simple interactive UI** where users can type text and update the label dynamically.

---

# *Creating Menus in Tkinter*

Menus provide navigation and **additional functionality** in GUI applications.

```
python

import tkinter as tk
from tkinter import messagebox

# Function for menu action
def show_about():
```

```
    messagebox.showinfo("About",   "This   is   a
Tkinter app!")

# Create main window
root = tk.Tk()
root.title("Tkinter Menu Example")

# Create a menu bar
menu_bar = tk.Menu(root)

# Create a "File" menu
file_menu = tk.Menu(menu_bar, tearoff=0)
file_menu.add_command(label="Open")
file_menu.add_command(label="Save")
file_menu.add_separator()
file_menu.add_command(label="Exit",
command=root.quit)

# Create a "Help" menu
help_menu = tk.Menu(menu_bar, tearoff=0)
help_menu.add_command(label="About",
command=show_about)

# Add menus to menu bar
menu_bar.add_cascade(label="File",
menu=file_menu)
menu_bar.add_cascade(label="Help",
menu=help_menu)

# Configure the window to use the menu
root.config(menu=menu_bar)

# Run application
root.mainloop()
```

# *Explanation*

- **Menu()** creates a menu bar.
- **add_command()** adds menu items.
- **messagebox.showinfo()** displays a popup window.

This example adds **File and Help menus**, improving navigation in the Tkinter app.

## Packaging a Tkinter App for Windows, macOS, and Linux

Once the GUI application is complete, it needs to be **packaged into an executable** so that users can run it without installing Python.

# *1. Using PyInstaller for Cross-Platform Packaging*

`PyInstaller` converts Python scripts into standalone executables. Install it with:

bash

```
pip install pyinstaller
```
*Windows: Creating an .exe File*
bash

```
pyinstaller --onefile --windowed my_app.py
```

- **--onefile**: Creates a single executable file.
- **--windowed**: Hides the terminal window.
- The output will be in the `dist/` folder (`my_app.exe`).

*macOS: Creating a .app File*
bash

```
pyinstaller --onefile --windowed --name "MyApp"
my_app.py
```

This creates a **macOS app bundle** (`MyApp.app`) that users can run directly.

*Linux: Creating an Executable Binary*
```
bash
```

```
pyinstaller --onefile my_app.py
```

This generates a **Linux binary** (`my_app`), which can be executed with:

```
bash
```

```
./dist/my_app
```

# 2. Creating an Installable Package

For better distribution, package the app using `cx_Freeze` or `py2app`.

### Windows: Creating an Installer

```
bash
```

```
pip install cx_Freeze
python setup.py build
```

### macOS: Creating a macOS .dmg Package

```
bash
```

```
pip install py2app
python setup.py py2app
```

This generates a **macOS installable application**.

## Conclusion

Tkinter is an excellent choice for **simple, cross-platform GUI applications**. While not as advanced as PyQt or Kivy, it remains **lightweight, easy to use, and natively included in Python**.

# *Key Takeaways*

- **Tkinter is built into Python**, making it ideal for **lightweight cross-platform apps**.
- **Widgets like labels, buttons, and menus** help create **interactive user interfaces**.
- **Packaging with PyInstaller** allows **standalone executables** to run on Windows, macOS, and Linux.

## What's Next?

In **Chapter 8**, we will explore:

- Building **advanced GUI applications with PyQt and PySide**.
- Handling **event-driven programming** for responsive UIs.
- Packaging and deploying **PyQt-based applications** across platforms.

By **understanding Tkinter**, developers can **build functional cross-platform applications quickly**, making it a great starting point for Python GUI programming.

This chapter **provides hands-on examples for Tkinter development** and **step-by-step instructions for cross-platform packaging**.!

# Chapter 8

# Creating Advanced GUIs with PyQt and PySide

While Tkinter is great for simple GUI applications, **PyQt and PySide** offer **modern, feature-rich, and scalable solutions** for professional-grade cross-platform applications. Both are based on the **Qt framework**, which is widely used for developing **high-performance, native-looking desktop applications**.

This chapter explores:

1. **Using Qt Designer** for rapid UI design
2. **Handling events and signals** to make applications interactive
3. **Packaging PyQt/PySide applications** for Windows, macOS, and Linux

---

## Understanding PyQt and PySide

PyQt and PySide are **bindings** for the Qt framework, providing access to Qt's powerful UI components in Python.

# PyQt vs. PySide: What's the Difference?

| Feature | PyQt | PySide |
|---|---|---|
| License | GPL or Commercial | LGPL (more permissive) |
| Maintained by | Riverbank Computing | The Qt Company |
| Features | Full Qt functionality | Full Qt functionality |
| Best for | Commercial & Open-Source Apps | LGPL-licensed apps |

**Which one to choose?**

- **Use PyQt** if you plan to buy a **commercial license** or develop **open-source applications** under GPL.
- **Use PySide** if you want an **LGPL-licensed alternative**, allowing closed-source apps without paying for a license.

Both **offer the same Qt features**, so the choice depends mainly on **licensing requirements**.

---

# Using Qt Designer for UI Design

Instead of writing GUI code manually, **Qt Designer** allows developers to **drag and drop UI components** to design applications visually.

## *Installing Qt Designer*

1. **Install PyQt5 and Qt Designer**

```
bash

pip install PyQt5 pyqt5-tools
```

On Linux/macOS:

```
bash

sudo apt install qttools5-dev-tools
```

2. **Open Qt Designer**
   - **Windows**: Run `designer.exe` from the PyQt5 installation directory.
   - **Linux/macOS**: Run `designer` from the terminal.

# Creating a UI with Qt Designer

1. Open Qt Designer and create a **Main Window** or **Dialog UI**.
2. Drag and drop **buttons, labels, input fields**, etc.
3. Save the file as `my_ui.ui`.

# Converting `.ui` Files to Python Code

After designing a UI, convert it to a Python script using:

```
bash

pyuic5 -x my_ui.ui -o my_ui.py  # PyQt
pyside6-uic my_ui.ui -o my_ui.py  # PySide
```

Now, `my_ui.py` can be imported and used in a Python project.

91

# Handling Events and Signals in PyQt/PySide

Qt uses **signals and slots** for event-driven programming. A **signal** is an event (e.g., button click), and a **slot** is a function that responds to that event.

## *Example: Connecting a Button to a Function*

python

```python
from PyQt5.QtWidgets import QApplication, QMainWindow, QPushButton

class MyApp(QMainWindow):
    def __init__(self):
        super().__init__()
        self.setWindowTitle("PyQt Signals and Slots")
        self.setGeometry(100, 100, 400, 300)

        # Create a button
        self.button = QPushButton("Click Me", self)
        self.button.setGeometry(150, 100, 100, 40)

        # Connect button click signal to a function (slot)

self.button.clicked.connect(self.on_button_click)

    def on_button_click(self):
        print("Button Clicked!")

# Run the application
```

92

```
app = QApplication([])
window = MyApp()
window.show()
app.exec_()
```

# *Explanation*

- `clicked.connect(self.on_button_click)`:
  Connects the **button click signal** to the
  `on_button_click` method.
- `self.setGeometry(100, 100, 400, 300)`: Sets the
  window size and position.
- `app.exec_()`: Starts the event loop.

This ensures that **GUI elements respond dynamically to
user interactions**.

## Packaging PyQt/PySide Applications for Distribution

After building a PyQt/PySide application, package it into an
**executable file** so that users can run it without needing
Python installed.

# *Using PyInstaller for Cross-Platform Packaging*

Install PyInstaller:

```
bash
```

```
pip install pyinstaller
```

# *Creating an Executable for Windows*

```bash
pyinstaller --onefile --windowed my_app.py
```

- **--onefile**: Creates a **single executable file**.
- **--windowed**: Hides the console window.

The output is in the dist/ folder (my_app.exe).

# *Creating an Executable for macOS*

```bash
pyinstaller --onefile --windowed --name "MyApp" my_app.py
```

This generates a **macOS .app bundle**.

# *Creating an Executable for Linux*

```bash
pyinstaller --onefile my_app.py
```

This generates a **Linux binary (my_app)**, which can be executed with:

```bash
./dist/my_app
```

# *Advanced Packaging with cx_Freeze (Optional)*

For more control over packaging, use **cx_Freeze**:

1. Install cx_Freeze:

   bash

   ```
   pip install cx_Freeze
   ```

2. Create a setup.py script:

   python

   ```
   from cx_Freeze import setup, Executable

   setup(
       name="MyApp",
       version="1.0",
       description="A PyQt Application",
       executables=[Executable("my_app.py")]
   )
   ```

3. Run:

   bash

   ```
   python setup.py build
   ```

This creates a **platform-specific executable**.

## Conclusion

PyQt and PySide provide **powerful, cross-platform GUI solutions** with modern UI components and event-driven programming. Using **Qt Designer** simplifies UI development, and **packaging with PyInstaller or cx_Freeze** ensures that applications can be distributed without requiring Python.

## *Key Takeaways*

- **Qt Designer** speeds up UI development using a drag-and-drop interface.
- **Signals and slots** handle user interactions dynamically.
- **PyInstaller and cx_Freeze** package PyQt/PySide applications for distribution on Windows, macOS, and Linux.

## What's Next?

In **Chapter 9**, we will explore:

- **Kivy for mobile-friendly applications**.
- **Building multi-touch, gesture-based interfaces**.
- **Deploying Kivy apps on Android and iOS**.

With **PyQt/PySide**, developers can build **high-performance, professional GUI applications** that work across multiple platforms.

This chapter **provides practical, hands-on knowledge** for **creating advanced GUI applications with PyQt and PySide**.

# Chapter 9

# *Web-Based Cross-Platform Applications*

Web applications have become the **most universal cross-platform solution**, allowing users to access software through a web browser without the need for installation. **Python's web frameworks**—Flask, Django, and FastAPI—offer powerful tools for building scalable, cross-platform web applications.

This chapter explores:

1. **Why web applications are the best cross-platform solution**
2. **Overview of Flask, Django, and FastAPI**
3. **Choosing between server-side and client-side rendering**

## Why Web Applications Are the Most Universal Cross-Platform Solution

Unlike traditional **desktop applications**, web applications do not depend on **operating system compatibility**, making them **accessible on any device** with a web browser.

## *Advantages of Web Applications for Cross-Platform Development*

- **No installation required** – Runs on a browser without platform-specific dependencies.
- **Universal accessibility** – Works on **Windows, macOS, Linux, Android, iOS**, and even smart TVs.
- **Easier updates and maintenance** – Updates are made on the server, eliminating the need for users to download updates.
- **Scalability** – Easily scaled from a **single-user app to millions of users** with cloud hosting.

# *When Not to Use Web Applications*

- **Offline functionality is critical** – Web apps need an internet connection, while native applications can work offline.
- **High-performance needs** – Web apps rely on internet speed, whereas native apps can directly access system resources.
- **Device-specific features** – If an application requires deep OS integration (e.g., low-level system access, GPU optimization), native development might be a better choice.

Despite these limitations, **web applications remain the best choice** for most cross-platform use cases.

# Overview of Flask, Django, and FastAPI

Python provides **three major web frameworks** for building cross-platform applications:

| Feature | Flask | Django | FastAPI |
|---|---|---|---|
| Type | Micro-framework | Full-stack framework | Asynchronous API framework |
| Ease of Use | Simple | Moderate | Moderate |
| Performance | Good | Slower | High-speed (async) |
| Best Use Cases | Small to medium apps, APIs | Large-scale applications | High-performance APIs, AI services |

Each framework is suited to **different types of web applications**.

---

# *Flask: The Lightweight Micro-Framework*

Flask is a **minimalist framework** for web applications that provides only **the essentials**, allowing developers to **add features as needed**.

*Installing Flask*
```bash
bash

pip install flask
```
*Basic Flask Application*
```python
python

from flask import Flask
```

```
app = Flask(__name__)

@app.route("/")
def home():
    return "Hello, Flask!"

if __name__ == "__main__":
    app.run(debug=True)
```

*Best Use Cases for Flask*

- **Simple web applications**
- **APIs and microservices**
- **Prototyping and lightweight web apps**

# *Django: The Full-Stack Web Framework*

Django is a **high-level web framework** that includes **built-in authentication, database management, and security features**.

*Installing Django*
```
bash
```

```
pip install django
```
*Creating a Django Project*
```
bash
```

```
django-admin startproject myproject
cd myproject
python manage.py runserver
```
*Django's Strengths*

- **Built-in authentication and security**

- **ORM (Object-Relational Mapping) for database management**
- **Admin interface for managing application data**

*Best Use Cases for Django*

- **Enterprise applications**
- **E-commerce platforms**
- **Data-driven applications**

# *FastAPI: The High-Performance API Framework*

FastAPI is an **asynchronous web framework** designed for **speed, performance, and efficiency**, making it ideal for APIs and AI-powered applications.

*Installing FastAPI*
```
bash

pip install fastapi uvicorn
```
*Basic FastAPI Application*
```python

from fastapi import FastAPI

app = FastAPI()

@app.get("/")
def home():
    return {"message": "Hello, FastAPI!"}

if __name__ == "__main__":
    import uvicorn
```

```
uvicorn.run(app,          host="127.0.0.1",
port=8000)
```

*FastAPI's Strengths*

- **Asynchronous support for high performance**
- **Automatic API documentation**
- **Ideal for real-time applications and machine learning APIs**

*Best Use Cases for FastAPI*

- **High-performance APIs**
- **AI/ML services**
- **Microservices and serverless applications**

# Choosing Between Server-Side vs Client-Side Rendering

Web applications can be rendered **on the server (server-side rendering) or in the browser (client-side rendering)**.

## *Server-Side Rendering (SSR)*

- **Rendering happens on the server** before sending HTML to the client.
- **Pros:**
  - Faster initial page load
  - Better for SEO
  - Works on low-power devices
- **Cons:**
  - Requires a page reload for every interaction
  - More server processing

*Example of Server-Side Rendering with Flask*
python

```
from flask import Flask, render_template

app = Flask(__name__)

@app.route("/")
def home():
    return render_template("index.html")

if __name__ == "__main__":
    app.run(debug=True)
```

# *Client-Side Rendering (CSR)*

- **Rendering happens in the browser** using JavaScript frameworks (e.g., React, Vue, Angular).
- **Pros:**
  - Smoother, interactive UI
  - Faster navigation between pages
  - Reduces server load
- **Cons:**
  - Slower first load time
  - Heavily dependent on JavaScript
  - May have SEO challenges

*Example: FastAPI with a React Frontend*
python

```
from fastapi import FastAPI
from      fastapi.middleware.cors      import
CORSMiddleware

app = FastAPI()

app.add_middleware(
    CORSMiddleware,
```

104

```
    allow_origins=["*"],
    allow_credentials=True,
    allow_methods=["*"],
    allow_headers=["*"],
)

@app.get("/api/data")
def get_data():
    return {"message": "Data from FastAPI"}
```

In this setup, the **backend serves APIs**, while **React handles frontend rendering**.

# Which Rendering Method Should You Choose?

| Requirement | Best Choice |
|---|---|
| SEO-friendly content | Server-Side Rendering (Flask/Django) |
| Interactive, fast UI | Client-Side Rendering (React/Vue with FastAPI) |
| Low server load | Client-Side Rendering |
| Faster initial load time | Server-Side Rendering |

For **hybrid applications**, use **SSR for SEO-critical pages** and **CSR for interactive sections**.

# Conclusion

Web applications are the **best cross-platform solution**, and Python provides three powerful frameworks—**Flask, Django, and FastAPI**—for building them.

## *Key Takeaways*

- **Flask** is great for **lightweight apps and APIs**.
- **Django** is ideal for **large-scale applications**.
- **FastAPI** is the best choice for **high-performance APIs**.
- **Server-side rendering** is best for SEO and content-heavy sites.
- **Client-side rendering** is ideal for **interactive, modern web applications**.

## What's Next?

In **Chapter 11**, we will:

- Build a **cross-platform web application using Flask**.
- Create **dynamic pages with templates**.
- Deploy Flask applications on **Heroku, AWS, and Google Cloud**.

Understanding **cross-platform web development** is essential for building **scalable, universally accessible applications**.

# Chapter 10

# Developing Mobile-Friendly Apps with Kivy

With the increasing demand for **cross-platform mobile applications**, Python developers can use **Kivy** to create **interactive, touch-friendly apps** that run on **Windows, macOS, Linux, Android, and iOS**. Kivy provides a **powerful UI framework**, allowing developers to design applications with **custom graphics, animations, and gesture support**.

This chapter explores:

1. **Introduction to Kivy and KV language**
2. **Creating responsive UIs for Android and iOS**
3. **Deploying a Kivy app on mobile devices**

## Introduction to Kivy and KV Language

# What is Kivy?

Kivy is an **open-source, cross-platform UI framework** designed for:

- **Touch-based applications** (supports gestures and multi-touch).
- **Modern UI with animations and graphics**.
- **Multi-platform compatibility** (runs on Windows, macOS, Linux, Android, and iOS).

107

# *Why Use Kivy?*

- **Write once, run anywhere** – A single codebase works on desktop and mobile.
- **Built-in touch and gesture support** – Ideal for mobile interfaces.
- **GPU acceleration** – Uses OpenGL for fast rendering.
- **Lightweight and flexible** – Works well for both simple and complex applications.

# *Installing Kivy*

Install Kivy using `pip`:

bash

```
pip install kivy
```

For mobile development, additional dependencies are needed.

- **For Windows/macOS/Linux development:**

  bash

  ```
  pip install kivy[full]
  ```

- **For Android deployment:**

  bash

  ```
  pip install python-for-android
  ```

- **For iOS deployment:**

  bash

108

```
pip install kivy-ios
```

# *Understanding KV Language*

Kivy provides a special **declarative language** called **KV language** to define UI layouts separately from Python logic. This makes the code **cleaner and more readable**.

*Basic KV Language Example*
```
kv

BoxLayout:
    orientation: "vertical"

    Label:
        text: "Welcome to Kivy!"
        font_size: 24

    Button:
        text: "Click Me"
        on_press: app.on_button_click()
```

This **defines a UI layout** with a **label and button** inside a vertical box layout.

*Using KV Language in a Python App*
```
python

from kivy.app import App
from kivy.uix.boxlayout import BoxLayout
from kivy.uix.label import Label
from kivy.uix.button import Button

class MyApp(App):
    def build(self):
        layout                            =
BoxLayout(orientation='vertical')
```

109

```
        self.label   =   Label(text="Welcome   to
Kivy!", font_size=24)
        button = Button(text="Click Me")

button.bind(on_press=self.on_button_click)

        layout.add_widget(self.label)
        layout.add_widget(button)
        return layout

    def on_button_click(self, instance):
        self.label.text = "Button Clicked!"

# Run the app
if __name__ == "__main__":
    MyApp().run()
```

# *Explanation*

- **BoxLayout** organizes UI elements vertically.
- **Label** displays text, and **Button** allows user interaction.
- **bind(on_press=self.on_button_click)** connects a button click event to the function on_button_click().

---

# Creating Responsive UIs for Android and iOS

# *1. Using Layouts for Responsive Design*

Kivy provides multiple **layout managers** to create dynamic UIs:

- **BoxLayout** – Arranges widgets vertically or horizontally.
- **GridLayout** – Organizes widgets in a grid.
- **FloatLayout** – Allows absolute positioning.
- **AnchorLayout** – Centers widgets.

*Example: GridLayout for Responsive Design*
kv

```
GridLayout:
    cols: 2
    Button:
        text: "Button 1"
    Button:
        text: "Button 2"
    Button:
        text: "Button 3"
    Button:
        text: "Button 4"
```

This layout ensures that buttons **resize dynamically** based on the screen size.

# 2. Adding Touch and Gesture Support

Kivy allows **multi-touch and gesture-based interactions**, making apps feel more like **native mobile applications**.

*Example: Gesture-Based Navigation*
python

```
from kivy.app import App
from kivy.uix.label import Label
from kivy.uix.floatlayout import FloatLayout
from kivy.core.window import Window

class GestureApp(App):
    def build(self):
```

```
        self.label = Label(text="Swipe to change
text", font_size=24)
        layout = FloatLayout()
        layout.add_widget(self.label)

Window.bind(on_touch_move=self.on_swipe)
        return layout

    def on_swipe(self, window, touch):
        if touch.dx > 50:   # Swipe right
            self.label.text = "Swiped Right!"
        elif touch.dx < -50:   # Swipe left
            self.label.text = "Swiped Left!"

if __name__ == "__main__":
    GestureApp().run()
```

# *Explanation*

- **Window.bind(on_touch_move=self.on_swipe)** detects swiping movements.
- **Changes the label text when the user swipes left or right.**

This enhances **user interaction**, making apps **more mobile-friendly**.

---

# Deploying a Kivy App on Mobile Devices

# *1. Packaging for Android with Buildozer*

Kivy applications can be converted into **Android APKs** using **Buildozer**.

*Installing Buildozer*
bash

```
pip install buildozer
```
*Building an APK*

1. Navigate to the app's directory and initialize Buildozer:

```
bash

buildozer init
```

2. Edit the **buildozer.spec** file:
   o Set package.name = MyKivyApp
   o Set          source.include_exts          =
     py,png,jpg,kv,atlas
   o Set android.api = 30 (or latest API version)
3. Run the build command:

```
bash

buildozer -v android debug
```

4. The generated APK will be in the bin/ directory, ready for installation on an Android device.

---

# *2. Deploying to iOS with Kivy-iOS*

For iOS, use kivy-ios to create an **Xcode project** and compile the app for iPhones and iPads.

*Setting Up Kivy for iOS*
bash

```
pip install kivy-ios
```

*Building the iOS App*

1. Create an iOS project:

   bash

   ```
   kivy-ios create myapp
   ```

2. Navigate into the project folder:

   bash

   ```
   cd myapp
   ```

3. Compile for iOS:

   bash

   ```
   kivy-ios build
   ```

4. Open the project in Xcode and deploy it to an iPhone.

---

# Conclusion

Kivy allows **Python developers to build mobile-friendly applications** that work on **Android, iOS, and desktops** with a single codebase. Its **gesture-based, touch-responsive UI** makes it an excellent choice for **mobile app development**.

# *Key Takeaways*

- **Kivy's KV language** simplifies UI design.
- **Layouts like BoxLayout and GridLayout** ensure responsive UI.

- **Gesture detection** improves user interaction.
- **Buildozer and Kivy-iOS** package Kivy apps for mobile deployment.

# What's Next?

In **Chapter 10**, we will:

- **Explore web-based cross-platform applications.**
- **Compare Flask, Django, and FastAPI** for web development.
- **Learn how to choose between server-side vs client-side rendering.**

With **Kivy**, developers can create **mobile-friendly applications** with Python, eliminating the need for Java or Swift.

# Chapter 11

# Building a Cross-Platform Web App with Flask

Flask is a **lightweight, flexible, and powerful** web framework for building **cross-platform web applications and APIs** in Python. It is ideal for **small to medium-sized web applications**, providing **a simple structure** without unnecessary complexity.

This chapter explores:

1. **Setting up a Flask project**
2. **Handling routes, templates, and APIs**
3. **Deploying Flask applications on Heroku, AWS, and Google Cloud**

## Setting Up a Flask Project

## Installing Flask

Before starting, install Flask using `pip`:

```bash

pip install flask
```

## Creating a Flask Project

1. **Create a project directory**:

116

```bash
bash

mkdir flask_app && cd flask_app
```

## 2. Create a virtual environment (recommended):

```bash
bash

python -m venv venv
source venv/bin/activate  # macOS/Linux
venv\Scripts\activate  # Windows
```

## 3. Install Flask inside the virtual environment:

```bash
bash

pip install flask
```

## 4. Create a main application file (app.py):

```python
python

from flask import Flask

app = Flask(__name__)

@app.route("/")
def home():
    return "Hello, Flask!"

if __name__ == "__main__":
    app.run(debug=True)
```

## 5. Run the application:

```bash
bash

python app.py
```

117

6. Open a browser and go to **http://127.0.0.1:5000/**, where **"Hello, Flask!"** will be displayed.

## Handling Routes, Templates, and APIs

# *1. Creating Routes and Views*

Flask uses **routes** to define different pages in a web application.

```python
from flask import Flask

app = Flask(__name__)

@app.route("/")
def home():
    return "Welcome to My Flask App!"

@app.route("/about")
def about():
    return "About Page"

if __name__ == "__main__":
    app.run(debug=True)
```

- **@app.route("/")** defines the homepage (http://127.0.0.1:5000/).
- **@app.route("/about")** creates an "About" page (http://127.0.0.1:5000/about).

118

# 2. Using HTML Templates

Flask allows **dynamic content rendering** using **Jinja2 templates**.

1. **Create a `templates/` folder** in your project directory.
2. **Create an HTML template (`templates/index.html`)**:

```html
html

<!DOCTYPE html>
<html>
<head>
    <title>Flask App</title>
</head>
<body>
    <h1>Welcome to Flask</h1>
    <p>{{ message }}</p>
</body>
</html>
```

3. **Modify `app.py` to render this template**:

```python
python

from flask import Flask, render_template

app = Flask(__name__)

@app.route("/")
def home():
    return render_template("index.html",
message="This is a Flask web app!")

if __name__ == "__main__":
    app.run(debug=True)
```

- **render_template()** loads index.html.

119

- `{{ message }}` is replaced dynamically with the text **"This is a Flask web app!"**.

Now, when you visit `http://127.0.0.1:5000/`, you will see the rendered **HTML page** instead of plain text.

---

## 3. Creating a REST API with Flask

Flask can also be used to create **RESTful APIs** for web and mobile applications.

1. **Install Flask-RESTful**:

    bash

    ```
    pip install flask-restful
    ```

2. **Create an API (`api.py`)**:

    python

    ```
    from flask import Flask, jsonify
    from flask_restful import Api, Resource

    app = Flask(__name__)
    api = Api(app)

    class HelloWorld(Resource):
        def get(self):
            return jsonify({"message": "Hello,
    API!"})

    api.add_resource(HelloWorld, "/api/hello")

    if __name__ == "__main__":
        app.run(debug=True)
    ```

3. **Run the API and test it in the browser**:

```
arduino
```

```
http://127.0.0.1:5000/api/hello
```

o This returns JSON:

```
json
```

```
{"message": "Hello, API!"}
```

Flask APIs are **lightweight, fast, and easy to integrate** with **mobile and frontend frameworks**.

# Deploying Flask Applications on Heroku, AWS, and Google Cloud

## *1. Deploying on Heroku*

*Step 1: Install Heroku CLI*

Download and install from: Heroku CLI

*Step 2: Initialize a Git Repository*

```
bash
```

```
git init
git add .
git commit -m "Initial commit"
```

*Step 3: Create a requirements.txt File*

```
bash
```

```
pip freeze > requirements.txt
```

*Step 4: Add a `Procfile` for Deployment*

Create a **Procfile** (no extension) in the root directory:

makefile

```
web: gunicorn app:app
```
*Step 5: Deploy to Heroku*
bash

```
heroku login
heroku create my-flask-app
git push heroku master
heroku open
```

Now your **Flask app is live on Heroku**.

---

# *2. Deploying on AWS (Elastic Beanstalk)*

1. Install AWS CLI and Elastic Beanstalk CLI:

   bash

   ```
   pip install awsebcli --upgrade
   ```

2. Initialize an AWS Elastic Beanstalk project:

   bash

   ```
   eb init -p python-3.8 flask-app
   ```

3. Deploy the Flask app:

   bash

```
eb create flask-env
eb open
```

Your Flask app is now hosted on AWS.

---

# 3. Deploying on Google Cloud (App Engine)

1. Install Google Cloud SDK:

   ```bash
   gcloud init
   ```

2. Create an `app.yaml` file for deployment:

   ```yaml
   runtime: python38
   entrypoint: gunicorn -b :$PORT app:app
   ```

3. Deploy the Flask app:

   ```bash
   gcloud app deploy
   gcloud app browse
   ```

Your Flask app is now hosted on **Google Cloud App Engine**.

---

# Conclusion

Flask is **a powerful yet simple framework** for building **cross-platform web applications** and APIs. It provides **flexibility, ease of use, and scalability**, making it an excellent choice for **web development**.

## *Key Takeaways*

- **Flask is lightweight and easy to set up**.
- **Templates allow dynamic content rendering**.
- **Flask can be used to create REST APIs** for web and mobile apps.
- **Deploying on Heroku, AWS, or Google Cloud** makes applications publicly accessible.

# What's Next?

In **Chapter 12**, we will:

- **Learn how to build scalable web applications with Django**.
- **Understand Django's ORM and MVC architecture**.
- **Deploy Django applications for real-world use**.

With **Flask**, developers can create **cross-platform web applications and APIs quickly and efficiently**. Let me know if you'd like any refinements before moving to **Chapter 12: Using Django for Scalable Web Applications**!

# Chapter 12

# *Using Django for Scalable Web Applications*

Django is a **high-level, full-stack web framework** designed to help developers build **scalable, secure, and maintainable applications** quickly. It follows the **Model-View-Controller (MVC) architecture**, allowing for a **structured and efficient approach to web development**.

This chapter explores:

1. Introduction to Django's MVC architecture
2. Creating APIs with Django Rest Framework (DRF)
3. Best practices for deploying Django applications

# Introduction to Django's MVC Architecture

# *Why Use Django for Scalable Web Applications?*

Django is widely used for **large-scale, data-driven applications** because:

- **Follows the "batteries-included" philosophy** – Comes with built-in authentication, ORM, security, and an admin panel.

- **Follows the DRY principle ("Don't Repeat Yourself")** – Encourages reusable and maintainable code.
- **Scalable and secure** – Used by platforms like Instagram, Pinterest, and Mozilla.
- **Works well with databases** – Supports **PostgreSQL, MySQL, SQLite, and NoSQL databases**.

# Understanding Django's MVC Architecture

Django follows the **Model-View-Template (MVT) pattern**, which is similar to **MVC (Model-View-Controller)** but with slight differences.

- **Model**: Defines the database structure (similar to ORM in other frameworks).
- **View**: Handles user requests and retrieves data.
- **Template**: Renders the data into an HTML page.

*Example MVT Workflow*

1. **User requests a webpage** → Django's **view processes the request**.
2. **The view interacts with the model (database)** → Retrieves or updates data.
3. **The view renders the template** → Displays data dynamically.

# Setting Up a Django Project

*1. Installing Django*
bash

```
pip install django
```

*2. Creating a Django Project*
bash

```
django-admin startproject myproject
cd myproject
python manage.py runserver
```

Visit **http://127.0.0.1:8000/** to see the default Django welcome page.

*3. Creating a Django App*

Django applications are **modular components** inside a project.

bash

```
python manage.py startapp myapp
```

*4. Registering the App in settings.py*

Add "myapp" to INSTALLED_APPS:

python

```
INSTALLED_APPS = [
    "django.contrib.admin",
    "django.contrib.auth",
    "django.contrib.contenttypes",
    "django.contrib.sessions",
    "django.contrib.messages",
    "django.contrib.staticfiles",
    "myapp",
]
```

# *Creating a Simple Model and View*

*1. Defining a Model in* models.py
python

```python
from django.db import models

class Product(models.Model):
    name = models.CharField(max_length=100)
    price = models.DecimalField(max_digits=10, decimal_places=2)
    description = models.TextField()

    def __str__(self):
        return self.name
```

*2. Running Migrations to Create Database Tables*
bash

```bash
python manage.py makemigrations
python manage.py migrate
```

*3. Creating a View in* views.py
python

```python
from django.shortcuts import render
from .models import Product

def product_list(request):
    products = Product.objects.all()
    return render(request, "product_list.html", {"products": products})
```

*4. Creating a Template (*templates/product_list.html*)*
html

```html
<!DOCTYPE html>
<html>
<head>
    <title>Product List</title>
</head>
<body>
    <h1>Product List</h1>
    <ul>
```

```
        {% for product in products %}
            <li>{{   product.name   }}   -   ${{
product.price }}</li>
        {% endfor %}
    </ul>
</body>
</html>
```

*5. Defining a URL in urls.py*

python

```
from django.urls import path
from .views import product_list

urlpatterns = [
    path("products/",               product_list,
name="product_list"),
]
```

Now, visiting **http://127.0.0.1:8000/products/**
displays the product list dynamically.

# Creating APIs with Django Rest Framework (DRF)

Django Rest Framework (DRF) allows developers to **build scalable REST APIs** with Django.

*1. Install Django Rest Framework*

bash

```
pip install djangorestframework
```

*2. Add DRF to settings.py*

python

```
INSTALLED_APPS = [
    "rest_framework",
    "myapp",
```

129

```
]
```

*3. Creating an API in* `views.py`

python

```python
from rest_framework.response import Response
from rest_framework.decorators import api_view
from .models import Product

@api_view(["GET"])
def product_list_api(request):
    products  =  Product.objects.values("name",
"price", "description")
    return              Response({"products":
list(products)})
```

*4. Defining an API URL in* `urls.py`

python

```python
from django.urls import path
from .views import product_list_api

urlpatterns = [
    path("api/products/",       product_list_api,
name="product_list_api"),
]
```

*5. Testing the API*

Visit **http://127.0.0.1:8000/api/products/**, and it
returns JSON:

json

```json
{
    "products": [
        {"name":  "Laptop",  "price":  1200.00,
"description": "A high-end laptop"},
        {"name":   "Phone",   "price":   800.00,
"description": "A premium smartphone"}
    ]
}
```

# Using DRF Serializers for More Structured APIs

DRF provides **serializers** to format model data.

*1. Creating a Serializer (`serializers.py`)*

python

```
from rest_framework import serializers
from .models import Product

class
ProductSerializer(serializers.ModelSerializer):
    class Meta:
        model = Product
        fields = "__all__"
```

*2. Using the Serializer in Views*

python

```
from rest_framework.generics import ListAPIView
from .models import Product
from .serializers import ProductSerializer

class ProductListAPI(ListAPIView):
    queryset = Product.objects.all()
    serializer_class = ProductSerializer
```

*3. Updating `urls.py` for the API*

python

```
from django.urls import path
from .views import ProductListAPI

urlpatterns = [
    path("api/products/",
ProductListAPI.as_view(),
name="product_list_api"),
]
```

131

This structured approach makes **Django APIs more maintainable and scalable**.

---

## Best Practices for Deploying Django Applications

### *1. Using Gunicorn and Nginx*

```bash
bash
```

```bash
pip install gunicorn
gunicorn    myproject.wsgi:application    --bind
0.0.0.0:8000
```

### *2. Deploying Django on Heroku*

1. Install **Heroku CLI** and set up Git:

   ```bash
   bash
   ```

   ```bash
   git init
   git add .
   git commit -m "Initial commit"
   ```

2. Create a `requirements.txt`:

   ```bash
   bash
   ```

   ```bash
   pip freeze > requirements.txt
   ```

3. Create a `Procfile` (without extension):

   ```makefile
   makefile
   ```

132

```
web: gunicorn myproject.wsgi
```

4.  Deploy to Heroku:

```bash
heroku login
heroku create django-app
git push heroku master
heroku open
```

# Conclusion

Django is **an excellent framework for scalable web applications**. Its **built-in features, ORM, and security mechanisms** make it suitable for **large-scale, database-driven projects**.

## *Key Takeaways*

- **Django follows the Model-View-Template (MVT) pattern** for structured development.
- **Django Rest Framework (DRF) makes building APIs efficient.**
- **Deploying Django on Heroku, AWS, or cloud platforms ensures scalability.**

# What's Next?

In **Chapter 13**, we will:

- Explore **FastAPI for high-performance web applications.**
- Build an **async API with automatic documentation.**

- Deploy FastAPI applications using **Docker and Kubernetes**.

Let me know if you'd like any refinements before moving to **Chapter 13: FastAPI for High-Performance APIs**!

# Chapter 13

# FastAPI for High-Performance APIs

FastAPI is a **modern, high-performance web framework** for building APIs with Python. It is designed for **speed, scalability, and automatic documentation**, making it a great choice for **microservices, AI applications, and real-time systems**.

This chapter explores:

1. **Why FastAPI is great for scalable, async applications**
2. **Building and testing APIs with FastAPI**
3. **Deploying FastAPI apps using Docker and Kubernetes**

## Why FastAPI is Great for Scalable, Async Applications

FastAPI is built on **ASGI (Asynchronous Server Gateway Interface)**, making it faster than traditional frameworks like Flask and Django.

# Advantages of FastAPI

- **High performance** – Almost as fast as Node.js and Go.
- **Asynchronous support** – Uses Python's `async` and `await` for **non-blocking operations**.
- **Automatic API documentation** – Generates **Swagger UI and ReDoc** automatically.
- **Data validation** – Uses **Pydantic** for type validation.

- **Easy to scale** – Ideal for **microservices and serverless applications**.

## Building and Testing APIs with FastAPI

# *1. Installing FastAPI and Uvicorn*

Install FastAPI and Uvicorn (a high-performance ASGI server):

bash

```
pip install fastapi uvicorn
```

# *2. Creating a Simple FastAPI Application*

Create a new file **app.py** and add the following code:

python

```
from fastapi import FastAPI

app = FastAPI()

@app.get("/")
def home():
    return {"message": "Welcome to FastAPI!"}

if __name__ == "__main__":
    import uvicorn
    uvicorn.run(app,               host="127.0.0.1", port=8000)
```

136

*Running the API Server*
bash

```
python app.py
```

Open **http://127.0.0.1:8000/**, and you should see:

json

```
{"message": "Welcome to FastAPI!"}
```

# 3. FastAPI Automatic API Documentation

FastAPI automatically generates **interactive API documentation**.

- **Swagger                                            UI**:
  Open **http://127.0.0.1:8000/docs** for interactive API testing.
- **ReDoc**:
  Open **http://127.0.0.1:8000/redoc** for detailed API documentation.

# 4. Creating a RESTful API with Path Parameters

Modify **app.py** to define a **dynamic API route**:

python

```
@app.get("/user/{user_id}")
```

137

```
def get_user(user_id: int):
    return {"user_id": user_id, "message": "User
found"}
```

*Testing the API*

Visit **http://127.0.0.1:8000/user/5**, and it returns:

json

```
{"user_id": 5, "message": "User found"}
```

# 5. Handling Query Parameters

Add support for **query parameters**:

python

```
@app.get("/search/")
def search_items(q: str = None):
    return {"query": q}
```

Visit **http://127.0.0.1:8000/search/?q=FastAPI**, and
it returns:

json

```
{"query": "FastAPI"}
```

# 6. Creating a POST API with Request Body

Use **Pydantic models** to validate request data:

python

```
from pydantic import BaseModel

class User(BaseModel):
    name: str
    age: int

@app.post("/create-user/")
def create_user(user: User):
    return   {"message":   f"User   {user.name}
created!", "age": user.age}
```

*Testing the API using cURL or Postman*

```
json

POST http://127.0.0.1:8000/create-user/
Content-Type: application/json

{
    "name": "Alice",
    "age": 30
}
```

Response:

```
json

{"message": "User Alice created!", "age": 30}
```

# Deploying FastAPI Apps Using Docker and Kubernetes

FastAPI is lightweight and designed for **containerized environments**.

# *1. Creating a Dockerfile for FastAPI*

Create a `Dockerfile` in the project root:

```
dockerfile

FROM python:3.9

WORKDIR /app

COPY . /app

RUN pip install --no-cache-dir fastapi uvicorn

CMD ["uvicorn", "app:app", "--host", "0.0.0.0",
"--port", "8000"]
```

# 2. Building and Running the Docker Container

*Step 1: Build the Docker Image*
```
bash

docker build -t fastapi-app .
```
*Step 2: Run the Container*
```
bash

docker run -d -p 8000:8000 fastapi-app
```
*Step 3: Access the FastAPI Application*

Open **http://127.0.0.1:8000/** in a browser.

# 3. Deploying FastAPI on Kubernetes

Kubernetes provides **scalability and orchestration** for containerized applications.

*Step 1: Creating a Kubernetes Deployment File (deployment.yaml)*

yaml

```yaml
apiVersion: apps/v1
kind: Deployment
metadata:
  name: fastapi-deployment
spec:
  replicas: 3
  selector:
    matchLabels:
      app: fastapi
  template:
    metadata:
      labels:
        app: fastapi
    spec:
      containers:
      - name: fastapi-container
        image: fastapi-app:latest
        ports:
        - containerPort: 8000
```

*Step 2: Creating a Kubernetes Service (service.yaml)*

yaml

```yaml
apiVersion: v1
kind: Service
metadata:
  name: fastapi-service
spec:
  selector:
    app: fastapi
  ports:
    - protocol: TCP
      port: 80
      targetPort: 8000
  type: LoadBalancer
```

141

*Step 3: Deploy FastAPI on Kubernetes*

bash

```
kubectl apply -f deployment.yaml
kubectl apply -f service.yaml
```

After deployment, the FastAPI service will be accessible from **a public IP**.

---

# 4. Deploying FastAPI on Cloud Platforms

*Deploying on Heroku*

1. Install **Heroku CLI**

   bash

   ```
   heroku login
   ```

2. Create a **Procfile** for Heroku:

   less

   ```
   web: uvicorn app:app --host=0.0.0.0 --port=${PORT}
   ```

3. Deploy to Heroku:

   bash

   ```
   heroku create fastapi-app
   git push heroku master
   heroku open
   ```

*Deploying on AWS (Elastic Beanstalk)*

1.  Install AWS Elastic Beanstalk CLI:

```bash
pip install awsebcli --upgrade
```

2.  Deploy the FastAPI application:

```bash
eb init -p python-3.8 fastapi-app
eb create fastapi-env
```

# Conclusion

FastAPI is **one of the fastest Python web frameworks**, ideal for **scalable APIs, microservices, and async applications**. By **containerizing with Docker and orchestrating with Kubernetes**, it can be deployed **on cloud platforms** efficiently.

# *Key Takeaways*

- **FastAPI is designed for high-performance and async operations.**
- **Pydantic ensures data validation and type safety.**
- **Docker makes deployment portable and scalable.**
- **Kubernetes provides auto-scaling and management.**
- **FastAPI's automatic documentation simplifies API testing.**

## What's Next?

In **Chapter 14**, we will:

- Explore **cross-platform game development with Pygame**.
- Build an **interactive game using Python**.
- Learn how to **distribute games across different platforms**.

With **FastAPI**, developers can create **modern, scalable APIs** quickly and efficiently. Let me know if you'd like any refinements before moving to **Chapter 14: Cross-Platform Game Development with Pygame**!

# Chapter 14

# *Cross-Platform Game Development with Pygame*

Python is a great language for game development, and **Pygame** is one of the most popular libraries for building **2D games** that run on **Windows, macOS, and Linux**. It provides tools for **graphics, sound, and event handling**, making it ideal for beginners and indie game developers.

This chapter explores:

1. **Introduction to game development with Python**
2. **Creating a simple game loop in Pygame**
3. **Packaging Pygame apps for different platforms**

## Introduction to Game Development with Python

Game development involves **handling user input, rendering graphics, updating game states, and playing sounds**. Python, despite being slower than C++ or Java, is widely used for:

- **2D games and prototyping**
- **Educational and casual games**
- **AI-driven game simulations**

# *Why Use Pygame?*

145

- **Cross-platform** – Runs on **Windows, macOS, and Linux**.
- **Beginner-friendly** – Simple API for handling graphics, input, and sound.
- **Lightweight and efficient** – Great for 2D game development.
- **Open-source** – Free to use for commercial and personal projects.

## Setting Up Pygame

### *1. Installing Pygame*

bash

```
pip install pygame
```

### *2. Creating a Basic Pygame Window*

Create a new file **game.py** and add the following:

python

```
import pygame

# Initialize Pygame
pygame.init()

# Set up the game window
WIDTH, HEIGHT = 800, 600
screen    =    pygame.display.set_mode((WIDTH,
HEIGHT))
pygame.display.set_caption("My First Pygame")

# Main game loop
running = True
while running:
```

146

```
    for event in pygame.event.get():
        if event.type == pygame.QUIT:   # Close
window event
            running = False

    screen.fill((30, 30, 30))  # Fill screen with
dark gray
    pygame.display.update()  # Refresh the screen

# Quit Pygame
pygame.quit()
```

*Explanation:*

- **pygame.init()** – Initializes all Pygame modules.
- **pygame.display.set_mode()** – Creates a game window.
- **pygame.event.get()** – Listens for events (e.g., keyboard, mouse, quit).
- **screen.fill(color)** – Fills the screen with a solid color.
- **pygame.display.update()** – Refreshes the display.

# Creating a Simple Game Loop in Pygame

A **game loop** continuously updates the game state and renders graphics.

## *Adding a Moving Object*

Modify **game.py** to include a **player-controlled object**:

```python
import pygame

# Initialize Pygame
```

147

```
pygame.init()

# Set up the game window
WIDTH, HEIGHT = 800, 600
screen     =     pygame.display.set_mode((WIDTH,
HEIGHT))
pygame.display.set_caption("Simple Pygame Loop")

# Define colors
WHITE = (255, 255, 255)
BLUE = (0, 0, 255)

# Define player properties
player_size = 50
player_x = WIDTH // 2 - player_size // 2
player_y = HEIGHT - 100
player_speed = 5

# Game loop
running = True
while running:
    screen.fill(WHITE)  # Clear screen

    for event in pygame.event.get():
        if event.type == pygame.QUIT:
            running = False

    # Get pressed keys
    keys = pygame.key.get_pressed()
    if keys[pygame.K_LEFT] and player_x > 0:
        player_x -= player_speed
    if keys[pygame.K_RIGHT] and player_x < WIDTH
- player_size:
        player_x += player_speed

    # Draw player
    pygame.draw.rect(screen,  BLUE,  (player_x,
player_y, player_size, player_size))

    pygame.display.update()

pygame.quit()
```

*Explanation:*

- Uses **arrow keys** to move a blue square.
- `pygame.key.get_pressed()` detects key presses.
- The **player moves left/right** based on key input.

Now, the player **can interact with the game**, making it a **simple but functional Pygame loop**.

# Adding Collision Detection and Enemy Movement

# *1. Adding an Enemy Object*

Modify `game.py` to include **a falling enemy block**:

```python
import pygame
import random

# Initialize Pygame
pygame.init()

# Set up game window
WIDTH, HEIGHT = 800, 600
screen     =     pygame.display.set_mode((WIDTH,
HEIGHT))
pygame.display.set_caption("Simple    Game    with
Collision")

# Colors
WHITE = (255, 255, 255)
BLUE = (0, 0, 255)
RED = (255, 0, 0)
```

```python
# Player properties
player_size = 50
player_x = WIDTH // 2 - player_size // 2
player_y = HEIGHT - 100
player_speed = 5

# Enemy properties
enemy_size = 50
enemy_x = random.randint(0, WIDTH - enemy_size)
enemy_y = 0
enemy_speed = 3

# Game loop
running = True
while running:
    screen.fill(WHITE)

    for event in pygame.event.get():
        if event.type == pygame.QUIT:
            running = False

    # Player movement
    keys = pygame.key.get_pressed()
    if keys[pygame.K_LEFT] and player_x > 0:
        player_x -= player_speed
    if keys[pygame.K_RIGHT] and player_x < WIDTH
- player_size:
        player_x += player_speed

    # Enemy movement
    enemy_y += enemy_speed
    if enemy_y > HEIGHT:
        enemy_y = 0
        enemy_x = random.randint(0, WIDTH -
enemy_size)

    # Collision detection
    if (player_x < enemy_x + enemy_size and
player_x + player_size > enemy_x and
            player_y < enemy_y + enemy_size and
player_y + player_size > enemy_y):
        print("Game Over!")
        running = False
```

```
# Draw objects
    pygame.draw.rect(screen,   BLUE,   (player_x,
player_y, player_size, player_size))
    pygame.draw.rect(screen,    RED,    (enemy_x,
enemy_y, enemy_size, enemy_size))

    pygame.display.update()

pygame.quit()
```

Now, a **red enemy block falls** and resets when it reaches the bottom. If the **player collides with the enemy**, the game prints **"Game Over!"** and exits.

# Packaging Pygame Apps for Different Platforms

To share a Pygame game, it must be **packaged into an executable file**.

## *1. Using PyInstaller for Cross-Platform Packaging*

*Windows: Creating an .exe File*
```
bash

pip install pyinstaller
pyinstaller --onefile --windowed game.py
```

- **--onefile**: Creates a **single executable file**.
- **--windowed**: Runs the game without a command line window.

*macOS: Creating a .app File*
```
bash

pyinstaller --onefile --windowed --name "MyGame"
game.py
```
*Linux: Creating an Executable Binary*
```
bash

pyinstaller --onefile game.py
```

Now, the game can run on **Windows, macOS, and Linux without requiring Python**.

## Conclusion

Pygame provides **an easy way to develop cross-platform 2D games** using Python. With **event handling, graphics, and sound support**, developers can **build interactive and engaging games**.

## *Key Takeaways*

- **Pygame simplifies game development in Python.**
- **Game loops handle user input, updates, and rendering.**
- **Collision detection enables interactive gameplay.**
- **PyInstaller packages games for different platforms.**

## What's Next?

In **Chapter 15**, we will:

- Explore **Godot and Unity for Python game development**.

- Learn how to **integrate Python scripting into game engines**.
- Deploy games for **Windows, macOS, Linux, Android, and iOS**.

With **Pygame**, developers can **easily build and distribute cross-platform 2D games**. Let me know if you'd like any refinements before moving to **Chapter 15: Using Godot and Unity for Python Game Development**!

# Chapter 15

# Using Godot and Unity for Python Game Development

While **Pygame** is great for **2D game development**, modern game engines like **Godot and Unity** provide advanced tools for **3D graphics, physics, animations, and multi-platform exports**. Developers can **integrate Python scripting** with these engines to create more sophisticated games.

This chapter explores:

1. **Overview of Godot and Unity with Python scripting**
2. **Integrating Python with game engines**
3. **Exporting games for Windows, macOS, Linux, Android, and iOS**

---

## Overview of Godot and Unity with Python Scripting

# Why Use a Game Engine Instead of Pygame?

- **Built-in physics and rendering** – Handles 2D/3D rendering and physics without extra code.
- **Optimized for performance** – Faster than Pygame for large-scale games.
- **Multi-platform support** – Export to Windows, macOS, Linux, Android, iOS, and even WebGL.

154

- **Integrated UI and tools** – Provides built-in editors, shaders, and asset management.

# 1. Godot Engine with Python (GDScript and PyGodot)

**Godot** is an **open-source** game engine designed for **2D and 3D game development**.

- **Lightweight and easy to use**.
- **Supports Python scripting** via **PyGodot** or **GDScript (similar to Python)**.
- **Built-in physics engine and animation tools**.

*Installing Godot*

Download Godot from the official site: ☞ https://godotengine.org/download

*Creating a Simple Godot Project*

1. **Open Godot** and create a new project.
2. **Add a Node2D** (right-click the Scene panel → "Add Node" → Select `Node2D`).
3. **Create a new GDScript file** for the node (`script.gd`).

```gdscript
extends Node2D

func _ready():
    print("Hello, Godot!")
```

155

4. **Run the scene** – The console prints "Hello, Godot!".

---

# *Integrating Python with Godot (PyGodot)*

Godot mainly uses **GDScript**, but you can integrate **Python using PyGodot**.

*Installing PyGodot*
bash

pip install pygodot
*Using Python in Godot*

1. **Enable Python support**: Go to **Project Settings** → **GDNative** → **Enable Python**.
2. **Create a Python script (`script.py`)**:

   ```python
   python

   from godot import exposed, export
   from godot.bindings import Node2D

   @exposed
   class MyPythonNode(Node2D):
       def _ready(self):
           print("Hello from Python!")
   ```

3. **Attach the Python script** to a **Node2D** in the Godot editor.
4. **Run the scene** – The console prints **"Hello from Python!"**.

---

# 2. Unity with Python (Unity-Py)

**Unity** is one of the most popular game engines, used for **AAA and indie game development**.

- **Supports 2D and 3D games** with **C# scripting**.
- **Python can be used for automation, AI, and game logic**.
- **Multi-platform support (PC, console, mobile, VR)**.

*Installing Unity*

Download Unity Hub from:
☞ https://unity.com/download

*Using Python in Unity (Unity-Py)*

1. Install the **Unity-Py** package:

   bash

   ```
   pip install unity-py
   ```

2. Create a **C# script in Unity** (`PythonIntegration.cs`):

   csharp

   ```
   using System.Diagnostics;
   using UnityEngine;

   public class PythonIntegration :
   MonoBehaviour
   {
       void Start()
       {
           Process.Start("python",
   "script.py");
       }
   ```

```
}
```

3. Create a **Python script (script.py)**:

```python
python

print("Hello from Python in Unity!")
```

4. Attach the **C# script to a GameObject** in Unity and **run the scene**.
5. The console prints **"Hello from Python in Unity!"**.

---

# Exporting Games for Windows, macOS, Linux, Android, and iOS

Both **Godot and Unity** allow **multi-platform exports** with a few clicks.

---

## *1. Exporting a Godot Game*

1. **Go to "Project" → "Export"**.
2. **Select a platform** (Windows, macOS, Linux, Android, Web, iOS).
3. **Set the export path and target**.
4. **Click "Export"** to generate the final game package.

---

## *2. Exporting a Unity Game*

1. **Go to "File" → "Build Settings"**.
2. **Select a platform** (PC, Mac, Linux, Android, iOS, WebGL).
3. **Click "Build"** to create an executable game file.

# *Conclusion*

Godot and Unity **offer advanced tools** for **cross-platform game development**, while **Python integration** allows for scripting and automation.

# *Key Takeaways*

- **Godot** is great for **2D/3D indie games** and supports **Python via PyGodot**.
- **Unity** is best for **large-scale 3D games** and integrates **Python for AI and automation**.
- **Both engines support multi-platform exports** for **PC, Mac, Linux, Android, and iOS**.

## What's Next?

In **Chapter 16**, we will:

- Explore **cross-platform automation with Python**.
- Learn **how to control Windows, macOS, and Linux using Python**.
- Use **automation tools like Selenium, PyAutoGUI, and Fabric**.

# Chapter 16

# Creating Cross-Platform Desktop Applications with Python

Building **cross-platform desktop applications** is a crucial use case for Python. Frameworks like **Tkinter, PyQt, and Kivy** provide tools to develop GUI-based applications that work on **Windows, macOS, and Linux**.

This chapter explores:

1. **Using Tkinter, PyQt, and Kivy for building cross-platform GUIs**
2. **Handling native OS integrations (file dialogs, notifications)**
3. **Real-world example: Developing a file organizer app with a GUI using PyQt**

---

# 1. Using Tkinter, PyQt, and Kivy for Cross-Platform GUIs

## Why Use Python for Desktop Applications?

- **Write once, run anywhere** – Works across Windows, macOS, and Linux.
- **Rich ecosystem** – Access to many libraries for file handling, automation, and UI design.

- **Lightweight** – Python GUI applications can be packaged as standalone executables.

# Comparison of Tkinter, PyQt, and Kivy

| Feature | Tkinter | PyQt | Kivy |
|---|---|---|---|
| **Ease of Use** | Easy | Moderate | Moderate |
| **Look & Feel** | Basic UI | Native-looking UI | Mobile-friendly UI |
| **Performance** | Lightweight | High | Medium |
| **Platform Support** | Windows, macOS, Linux | Windows, macOS, Linux | Windows, macOS, Linux, Android, iOS |
| **Best For** | Small utilities | Professional desktop apps | Touch-based applications |

# 1.1 Tkinter: The Built-in GUI Framework

**Pros:**

- Comes **pre-installed with Python**.
- Simple to learn and use.
- Works on all **major operating systems**.

161

## Cons:

- Outdated look and feel.
- Limited customization options.

### Example: Basic Tkinter App

```python
import tkinter as tk

root = tk.Tk()
root.title("Tkinter App")
root.geometry("300x200")

label = tk.Label(root, text="Hello, Tkinter!",
font=("Arial", 14))
label.pack(pady=20)

root.mainloop()
```

# 1.2 PyQt: The Professional Choice

## Pros:

- **Modern UI with rich widgets**.
- **Great for complex applications** (data visualization, multi-threading).
- **Supports drag-and-drop UI design** with Qt Designer.

## Cons:

- **Steeper learning curve** than Tkinter.
- **Commercial license required** for closed-source projects.

### Example: Basic PyQt App

```
python

from    PyQt5.QtWidgets    import    QApplication,
QLabel, QWidget

app = QApplication([])
window = QWidget()
window.setWindowTitle("PyQt App")
window.setGeometry(100, 100, 300, 200)

label = QLabel("Hello, PyQt!", window)
label.move(100, 80)

window.show()
app.exec_()
```

# *1.3 Kivy: For Touch-Based Interfaces*

## Pros:

- **Supports mobile development** (Android & iOS).
- **Multi-touch gestures and animations**.

## Cons:

- UI looks **less native on desktops**.
- Requires **separate dependencies** for mobile builds.

### Example: Basic Kivy App

```
python

from kivy.app import App
from kivy.uix.label import Label

class MyApp(App):
    def build(self):
        return Label(text="Hello, Kivy!")
```

```
MyApp().run()
```

# 2. Handling Native OS Integrations

## *2.1 File Dialogs*

*Tkinter File Dialog*
```
python

from tkinter import filedialog, Tk

root = Tk()
root.withdraw()   # Hide main window

file_path                                =
filedialog.askopenfilename(title="Select        a
file")
print("Selected file:", file_path)
```
*PyQt File Dialog*
```
python

from    PyQt5.QtWidgets    import    QApplication,
QFileDialog

app = QApplication([])
file_path, _ = QFileDialog.getOpenFileName(None,
"Select a file")
print("Selected file:", file_path)
```

## *2.2 System Notifications*

*Windows Notification (Using plyer)*
```
python

from plyer import notification
```

```
notification.notify(
    title="Reminder",
    message="Don't forget to check your email!",
    timeout=5
)
```

*macOS Notification (Using `osascript`)*

python

```
import os
os.system('osascript -e \'display notification
"Check your email!" with title "Reminder"\'')
```

*Linux Notification (Using `notify-send`)*

python

```
import os
os.system('notify-send "Reminder" "Check your
email!"')
```

# 3. Real-World Example: Developing a File Organizer App with PyQt

## *3.1 Project Overview*

This app will **scan a selected folder** and automatically **organize files into subfolders** based on their extensions (e.g., `.jpg`, `.pdf`, `.mp4`).

## *3.2 Installing Dependencies*

bash

```
pip install PyQt5
```

# 3.3 Implementing the File Organizer App

## Create `file_organizer.py`

```python
python

import os
import shutil
from PyQt5.QtWidgets import QApplication,
QWidget, QPushButton, QFileDialog, QLabel,
QVBoxLayout

class FileOrganizerApp(QWidget):
    def __init__(self):
        super().__init__()
        self.initUI()

    def initUI(self):
        self.setWindowTitle("File Organizer")
        self.setGeometry(100, 100, 400, 200)

        self.label = QLabel("Select a folder to
organize", self)

        self.button = QPushButton("Choose
Folder", self)

self.button.clicked.connect(self.choose_folder)

        layout = QVBoxLayout()
        layout.addWidget(self.label)
        layout.addWidget(self.button)

        self.setLayout(layout)

    def choose_folder(self):
        folder_path                           =
QFileDialog.getExistingDirectory(self,   "Select
Folder")
        if folder_path:
```

166

```
            self.label.setText(f"Organizing:
{folder_path}")
            self.organize_files(folder_path)

    def organize_files(self, folder_path):
        file_extensions = {
            "Images": [".jpg", ".jpeg", ".png",
".gif"],
            "Documents":    [".pdf",    ".docx",
".txt"],
            "Videos": [".mp4", ".mov", ".avi"],
            "Audio": [".mp3", ".wav"]
        }

        for              file_name              in
os.listdir(folder_path):
            file_path                            =
os.path.join(folder_path, file_name)
            if os.path.isfile(file_path):
                for  category,  extensions  in
file_extensions.items():
                    if
file_name.lower().endswith(tuple(extensions)):
                        category_folder      =
os.path.join(folder_path, category)

os.makedirs(category_folder, exist_ok=True)
                        shutil.move(file_path,
os.path.join(category_folder, file_name))

        self.label.setText("Files      Organized
Successfully!")

if __name__ == "__main__":
    app = QApplication([])
    window = FileOrganizerApp()
    window.show()
    app.exec_()
```

# *3.4 Running the App*

167

```bash
python file_organizer.py
```

Now, selecting a folder will **automatically categorize and move files** into appropriate subfolders.

---

# 4. Packaging the Application for Windows, macOS, and Linux

## *4.1 Using PyInstaller to Create an Executable*

Install **PyInstaller**:

```bash
pip install pyinstaller
```
*Windows: Creating an .exe File*
```bash
pyinstaller        --onefile        --windowed
file_organizer.py
```
*macOS: Creating a .app File*
```bash
pyinstaller    --onefile    --windowed    --name
"FileOrganizer" file_organizer.py
```
*Linux: Creating an Executable Binary*
```bash
pyinstaller --onefile file_organizer.py
```

The **packaged application** will be in the `dist/` folder.

# Conclusion

Python provides powerful tools to **develop cross-platform desktop applications**. **PyQt** is an excellent choice for **modern UI development**, while **Tkinter and Kivy** offer **alternative approaches**.

## *Key Takeaways*

- PyQt is great for professional desktop applications.
- Tkinter is simple and built into Python.
- Kivy supports mobile and touch-based UIs.
- File dialogs and system notifications improve user experience.
- Packaging with PyInstaller makes applications standalone.

# What's Next?

In **Chapter 17**, we will:

- Learn how to **use Python for cross-platform automation**.
- Automate **file management, system tasks, and browser interactions**.
- Explore tools like **Selenium, PyAutoGUI, and Fabric**.

# Chapter 16

# Choosing the Right Database for Cross-Platform Development

Databases are essential for storing, retrieving, and managing data in **cross-platform applications**. Choosing the right database depends on **scalability, performance, and data structure requirements**. Python provides excellent support for **both SQL and NoSQL databases**, making it easy to integrate databases into **desktop, web, and mobile applications**.

This chapter explores:

1. **SQL vs. NoSQL databases**
2. **Overview of SQLite, PostgreSQL, and MongoDB**
3. **Managing databases efficiently with SQLAlchemy**

---

## 1. SQL vs. NoSQL Databases

Databases are broadly categorized into **SQL (relational) and NoSQL (non-relational) databases**. The choice depends on **how the application stores and retrieves data**.

# SQL Databases (Structured Data Storage)

- Use **tables with predefined schemas**.
- Support **ACID (Atomicity, Consistency, Isolation, Durability)** transactions.

170

- Best for **structured data** with relationships (e.g., financial systems, e-commerce).

◆ **Examples: SQLite, PostgreSQL, MySQL**

# *NoSQL Databases (Unstructured & Scalable Data Storage)*

- Store data as **JSON, key-value pairs, or documents**.
- Support **horizontal scaling** for large-scale applications.
- Best for **big data, real-time analytics, and flexible schemas**.

◆ **Examples: MongoDB, Redis, Firebase**

# *Comparison: SQL vs. NoSQL*

| Feature | SQL (Relational) | NoSQL (Non-Relational) |
|---|---|---|
| Data Model | Tables with rows & columns | JSON, key-value, documents |
| Schema | Fixed schema | Flexible schema |
| Scalability | Vertical scaling | Horizontal scaling |
| Transactions | ACID-compliant | Eventual consistency |

| Feature | SQL (Relational) | NoSQL (Non-Relational) |
|---|---|---|
| Best For | Structured data | Unstructured, large-scale data |

# 2. Overview of SQLite, PostgreSQL, and MongoDB

## *2.1 SQLite: Lightweight Embedded SQL Database*

**Best for:** Small-scale applications, local storage, mobile apps.

◆ **Pros:**
No setup required (built into Python). Works offline with a local `.db` file. Ideal for mobile & lightweight applications.

◆ **Cons:**
Not suitable for high concurrency. No built-in user authentication.

*Installing and Using SQLite in Python*
python

```python
import sqlite3

# Connect to a database (or create it)
conn = sqlite3.connect("mydatabase.db")
cursor = conn.cursor()

# Create a table
```

```
cursor.execute("CREATE TABLE IF NOT EXISTS users
(id  INTEGER  PRIMARY  KEY,  name  TEXT,  age
INTEGER)")

# Insert data
cursor.execute("INSERT  INTO  users  (name,  age)
VALUES (?, ?)", ("Alice", 30))
conn.commit()

# Retrieve data
cursor.execute("SELECT * FROM users")
print(cursor.fetchall())

# Close the connection
conn.close()
```

# 2.2 PostgreSQL: The Scalable SQL Database

**Best for:** Large-scale applications, enterprise systems, cloud deployments.

◆ **Pros:**
Handles **high concurrency** efficiently. Supports **JSONB (hybrid SQL-NoSQL approach)**. Advanced security features.

◆ **Cons:**
Requires setup and database server. More complex than SQLite.

*Installing and Using PostgreSQL with Python*

1. Install PostgreSQL:

    ```bash
    sudo apt install postgresql   # Ubuntu
    brew install postgresql       # macOS
    ```

173

2. Install the `psycopg2` Python adapter:

bash

```
pip install psycopg2
```

3. **Connecting to PostgreSQL in Python**:

python

```
import psycopg2

conn = psycopg2.connect(database="mydb",
user="postgres", password="password",
host="localhost", port="5432")
cursor = conn.cursor()

cursor.execute("CREATE TABLE IF NOT EXISTS
users (id SERIAL PRIMARY KEY, name TEXT,
age INTEGER)")
cursor.execute("INSERT INTO users (name,
age) VALUES (%s, %s)", ("Bob", 25))
conn.commit()

cursor.execute("SELECT * FROM users")
print(cursor.fetchall())

conn.close()
```

# 2.3 MongoDB: The Flexible NoSQL Database

**Best for:** Large-scale, real-time, and unstructured data storage.

◆                                                      **Pros:**
Stores     data     as     **JSON**     **documents**.
Supports          **horizontal**               **scaling**.

174

Ideal for **real-time applications** (social media, IoT, AI).
♦ **Cons:**
Not ideal for complex transactions. Higher storage overhead than SQL databases.

*Installing and Using MongoDB with Python*

1.  Install MongoDB:

    bash

    ```
    sudo apt install mongodb   # Ubuntu
    brew install mongodb       # macOS
    ```

2.  Install the pymongo Python driver:

    bash

    ```
    pip install pymongo
    ```

3.  **Connecting to MongoDB in Python**:

    python

    ```
    from pymongo import MongoClient

    client =
    MongoClient("mongodb://localhost:27017/")
    db = client["mydatabase"]
    users_collection = db["users"]

    # Insert data
    users_collection.insert_one({"name":
    "Charlie", "age": 28})

    # Retrieve data
    for user in users_collection.find():
        print(user)
    ```

# 3. Managing Databases Efficiently with SQLAlchemy

SQLAlchemy is a powerful **Object-Relational Mapping (ORM)** library that provides:

- **Database independence** (works with SQLite, PostgreSQL, MySQL).
- **Easy model definition** (avoids raw SQL queries).
- **Improved code maintainability**.

## *3.1 Installing SQLAlchemy*

```bash
bash

pip install sqlalchemy
```

## *3.2 Creating a Database Model with SQLAlchemy*

```python
python

from sqlalchemy import create_engine, Column,
Integer, String
from        sqlalchemy.ext.declarative        import
declarative_base
from sqlalchemy.orm import sessionmaker

# Create an SQLite database (change URL for
PostgreSQL or MySQL)
DATABASE_URL = "sqlite:///mydatabase.db"
engine = create_engine(DATABASE_URL)
Base = declarative_base()

# Define a User model
```

176

```
class User(Base):
    __tablename__ = "users"
    id = Column(Integer, primary_key=True)
    name = Column(String)
    age = Column(Integer)

# Create tables
Base.metadata.create_all(engine)

# Create a session
Session = sessionmaker(bind=engine)
session = Session()

# Insert a new user
new_user = User(name="Alice", age=30)
session.add(new_user)
session.commit()

# Query users
users = session.query(User).all()
for user in users:
    print(user.name, user.age)
```

# 3.3 Switching Between Databases with SQLAlchemy

Change the DATABASE_URL to use **PostgreSQL** or **MySQL** without modifying the rest of the code:

```python
DATABASE_URL                              =
"postgresql://user:password@localhost/mydatabas
e"  # PostgreSQL
DATABASE_URL                              =
"mysql://user:password@localhost/mydatabase"  #
MySQL
DATABASE_URL = "sqlite:///mydatabase.db"  #
SQLite
```

SQLAlchemy makes it **easy to switch between databases**, making Python applications more **flexible and scalable**.

## Conclusion

Choosing the right database is **crucial** for application performance and scalability. **SQL databases** provide structured storage, while **NoSQL databases** handle flexible and large-scale data efficiently.

## *Key Takeaways*

- **SQLite** is best for **small applications** and **local storage**.
- **PostgreSQL** is ideal for **enterprise applications and cloud services**.
- **MongoDB** is perfect for **scalable, real-time applications**.
- **SQLAlchemy ORM** simplifies database management across different platforms.

## What's Next?

In **Chapter 17**, we will:

- Learn **how to sync databases across multiple devices**.
- Use **cloud-based database solutions like Firebase, AWS RDS, and Google Firestore**.
- Implement **real-time database updates** with Python.

Let me know if you'd like any refinements before moving to **Chapter 17: Syncing Databases Across Devices and Cloud!**

# Chapter 17

## Storing Data Locally vs in the Cloud

Storing data is a critical part of any **cross-platform application**, and developers must decide between **local storage** and **cloud-based databases** depending on their use case. This chapter explores **SQLite for local storage**, **cloud database solutions like Firebase, AWS DynamoDB, and Supabase**, and **best practices for secure data storage**.

---

# 1. Using SQLite for Local Storage

## Why Use Local Storage?

- Works **offline** without an internet connection.
- Best for **single-user applications** (e.g., note-taking apps, to-do lists).
- **Lightweight and embedded** (no separate database server required).

## Setting Up SQLite in Python

SQLite is **built into Python**, so no installation is needed.

```python
import sqlite3

# Connect to SQLite database (creates a file if
it doesn't exist)
conn = sqlite3.connect("local_data.db")
```

```
cursor = conn.cursor()

# Create a table
cursor.execute("""
    CREATE TABLE IF NOT EXISTS users (
        id INTEGER PRIMARY KEY AUTOINCREMENT,
        name TEXT NOT NULL,
        age INTEGER
    )
""")

# Insert data
cursor.execute("INSERT INTO users (name, age)
VALUES (?, ?)", ("Alice", 25))
conn.commit()

# Retrieve data
cursor.execute("SELECT * FROM users")
print(cursor.fetchall())

conn.close()
```

# *Pros & Cons of SQLite for Local Storage*

**Pros:**
No server required, **lightweight**.
**Fast and reliable** for single-user apps.
Cross-platform support (Windows, macOS, Linux, Android).

**Cons:**
**Not suitable for multi-user access**.
**No real-time synchronization** (cloud solutions needed for this).

181

# 2. Cloud-Based Databases: Firebase, AWS DynamoDB, and Supabase

## *Why Use Cloud Databases?*

- **Multi-device synchronization** (data updates across devices in real-time).
- **Scalability** (handles thousands/millions of users).
- **Better security and backups** (hosted by cloud providers).

---

## *2.1 Firebase: Real-Time NoSQL Database*

**Best for:** Mobile and web applications needing **real-time data sync**.

*Installing Firebase SDK for Python*
bash

```
pip install firebase-admin
```
*Setting Up Firebase in Python*

1. **Create a Firebase project** at Firebase Console.
2. **Download the serviceAccount.json key**.
3. **Initialize Firebase in Python**:

python

```
import firebase_admin
from firebase_admin import credentials, firestore
```

```
# Load credentials
cred                                           =
credentials.Certificate("serviceAccount.json")
firebase_admin.initialize_app(cred)

# Initialize Firestore database
db = firestore.client()

# Add data
doc_ref                                        =
db.collection("users").document("user_1")
doc_ref.set({"name": "Alice", "age": 25})

# Retrieve data
docs = db.collection("users").get()
for doc in docs:
    print(doc.id, doc.to_dict())
```

**Pros:**
**Real-time data updates** across multiple devices.
**Great for mobile/web apps**.

**Cons:**
**Limited free-tier usage**.
**Not the best for complex queries**.

# *2.2 AWS DynamoDB: Scalable NoSQL Database*

**Best for:** Large-scale applications requiring **high-performance NoSQL storage**.

*Installing AWS SDK for Python (Boto3)*
```
bash

pip install boto3
```

183

*Connecting to DynamoDB in Python*

```python
python

import boto3

# Initialize DynamoDB client
dynamodb       =       boto3.resource("dynamodb",
region_name="us-east-1")

# Create a table
table = dynamodb.create_table(
    TableName="Users",
    KeySchema=[{"AttributeName":          "id",
"KeyType": "HASH"}],
    AttributeDefinitions=[{"AttributeName":
"id", "AttributeType": "S"}],
    ProvisionedThroughput={"ReadCapacityUnits":
1, "WriteCapacityUnits": 1}
)

# Insert data
table.put_item(Item={"id":  "1",  "name":  "Bob",
"age": 30})

# Retrieve data
response = table.get_item(Key={"id": "1"})
print(response["Item"])
```

**Pros:**
**Highly    scalable**  (used   by   Amazon   services).
**Automatic backups and security**.

**Cons:**
**More   expensive   than   Firebase   or   SQLite**.
**Requires AWS setup**.

# 2.3 Supabase: Open-Source Firebase Alternative

**Best for:** Developers who want **Firebase-like features but self-hosted**.

*Installing Supabase SDK for Python*
bash

```
pip install supabase
```

*Connecting to Supabase in Python*

1. **Create a Supabase project** at Supabase.io.
2. **Get the API URL and Key**.
3. **Use Python to interact with Supabase**:

```python
python

from supabase import create_client

SUPABASE_URL = "https://xyzcompany.supabase.co"
SUPABASE_KEY = "your-api-key"
supabase      =      create_client(SUPABASE_URL,
SUPABASE_KEY)

# Insert data
data,                           _                    =
supabase.table("users").insert({"name":
"Charlie", "age": 28}).execute()

# Retrieve data
data,                           _                    =
supabase.table("users").select("*").execute()
print(data)
```

**Pros:**
**Open-source     alternative     to     Firebase.**
**Works with SQL (PostgreSQL backend).**

185

**Cons:**
**Still a newer platform** (not as mature as Firebase).

---

# 3. Best Practices for Secure Data Storage

Regardless of where data is stored, **security is essential**.

## *3.1 Encrypting Sensitive Data*

```python
from cryptography.fernet import Fernet

# Generate a key
key = Fernet.generate_key()
cipher = Fernet(key)

# Encrypt data
encrypted_data = cipher.encrypt(b"Sensitive
Information")
print("Encrypted:", encrypted_data)

# Decrypt data
decrypted_data = cipher.decrypt(encrypted_data)
print("Decrypted:", decrypted_data.decode())
```

 **Use Cases:** Encrypt **passwords, API keys, personal user data**.

---

## *3.2 Storing Credentials Securely*

- **NEVER hardcode credentials** in Python scripts.
- Use **environment variables** instead:

```python
python

import os

# Store credentials securely
os.environ["DATABASE_URL"]                        =
"postgresql://user:password@localhost/db"

# Retrieve credentials
db_url = os.getenv("DATABASE_URL")
print("Database URL:", db_url)
```

**Use Cases:** Hide **database passwords, API keys**.

# 3.3 Enforcing Authentication in Cloud Databases

- Use **Firebase Authentication** for user login.
- Use **IAM Roles in AWS DynamoDB** for secure access.
- Enable **SSL encryption** for database connections.

## Conclusion

Choosing between **local storage and cloud databases** depends on the application's needs.

**SQLite** – Best for **offline applications** and lightweight data storage.
**Firebase** – Best for **real-time apps** with multi-device sync.
**AWS DynamoDB** – Best for **enterprise-scale applications**.
**Supabase** – Open-source **Firebase alternative** for SQL users.

**Security is essential** – Always encrypt sensitive data, use environment variables, and enforce authentication.

# What's Next?

In **Chapter 18**, we will:

- **Sync databases across devices** using **real-time data streaming**.
- **Implement database backups and disaster recovery strategies**.
- **Use caching techniques (Redis, Memcached) to improve performance**.

# Chapter 18

# *Automating Tasks Across Platforms with Python*

Automation is one of **Python's greatest strengths**, allowing developers to create **portable scripts** that work across **Windows, macOS, and Linux**. By using **file management**, **system commands**, and **task scheduling**, Python can be leveraged to **automate repetitive tasks efficiently**.

This chapter explores:

1. Writing portable scripts for file management
2. Using the `subprocess` and `os` modules for system commands
3. Scheduling tasks with Cron (Linux/macOS) and Task Scheduler (Windows)

---

# 1. Writing Portable Scripts for File Management

File and folder operations are **essential for automation**, such as:

- **Organizing files** (e.g., sorting documents by type).
- **Cleaning up old files** (e.g., deleting temporary files).
- **Backing up important files**.

# *1.1 Cross-Platform File Operations*

Python's **os and shutil** modules provide a simple way to handle file operations across different operating systems.

*Example: Moving Files Based on Extensions*

```python
python

import os
import shutil

# Define source folder
source_folder = "/path/to/source"  # Change this
to the correct path

# Define file type categories
file_types = {
    "Documents": [".pdf", ".docx", ".txt"],
    "Images": [".jpg", ".jpeg", ".png"],
    "Videos": [".mp4", ".mov", ".avi"],
}

# Create category folders if they don't exist
for category in file_types.keys():
    os.makedirs(os.path.join(source_folder,
category), exist_ok=True)

# Move files into corresponding folders
for file_name in os.listdir(source_folder):
    file_path    =    os.path.join(source_folder,
file_name)

    if os.path.isfile(file_path):
        for    category,    extensions    in
file_types.items():
            if
file_name.lower().endswith(tuple(extensions)):
                shutil.move(file_path,
os.path.join(source_folder,            category,
file_name))

print("Files organized successfully!")
```

190

*Explanation:*

- Organizes **documents, images, and videos** into subfolders.
- Uses `shutil.move()` to **move files efficiently**.
- Works **on Windows, macOS, and Linux** without modification.

 **Use Case:** Automating file organization **in a downloads folder**.

---

# *1.2 Deleting Old Files Automatically*

Deleting **temporary files or log files** older than a certain period can free up **storage space**.

*Example: Deleting Files Older than 7 Days*

```python
import os
import time

folder_path = "/path/to/folder"  # Change this
path
days_to_keep = 7

# Convert days to seconds
time_threshold = time.time() - (days_to_keep *
86400)

# Iterate over files
for file_name in os.listdir(folder_path):
    file_path   =   os.path.join(folder_path,
file_name)

    if      os.path.isfile(file_path)       and
os.path.getmtime(file_path) < time_threshold:
```

```
    os.remove(file_path)
    print(f"Deleted: {file_name}")

print("Cleanup complete!")
```

**Use Case:** Automating **log file cleanup** for servers or local machines.

---

# 2. Using subprocess and os Modules for System Commands

## *2.1 Running System Commands*

The subprocess module allows **cross-platform execution** of system commands.

*Example: Checking Disk Space*
```python
python

import subprocess
import platform

# Determine OS and set command
if platform.system() == "Windows":
    command    =    "wmic    logicaldisk    get
size,freespace,caption"
else:
    command = "df -h"

# Run command
output   =   subprocess.run(command,   shell=True,
capture_output=True, text=True)
print(output.stdout)
```

**Use Case:** Automating **disk space monitoring**.

## *2.2 Copying Files Across Systems*

*Example: Copy a File to Another Directory*
python

```
import shutil

shutil.copy("source.txt", "destination_folder/")
print("File copied successfully!")
```

**Use Case:** Automating **file backups**.

# 3. Scheduling Tasks with Cron (Linux/macOS) and Task Scheduler (Windows)

## *3.1 Scheduling Python Scripts with Cron (Linux/macOS)*

Cron allows scheduling **Python scripts** to run at specific times.

*Example: Scheduling a Script to Run Every Day at Midnight*

1. **Open the crontab editor:**

   bash

   ```
   crontab -e
   ```

2. **Add a new cron job:**

```ruby
0    0    *    *    *    /usr/bin/python3
/path/to/script.py
```

**Use Case:** Running **daily automation scripts** like backups or reports.

# 3.2 Scheduling Python Scripts in Windows Task Scheduler

1. **Open Task Scheduler** and select **Create Basic Task**.
2. Choose **Trigger → Daily**.
3. Choose **Action → Start a program**.
4. Browse and select `python.exe` as the program.
5. In **Arguments**, add:

```swift
"C:\path\to\script.py"
```

**Use Case:** Automating **file backups, reports, or cleanup scripts**.

## Conclusion

Python makes **cross-platform automation** easy using **file operations, system commands, and scheduling**.

194

**Key Takeaways:**

- Use **os, shutil** for **file management**.
- Use **subprocess** to run **system commands**.
- Use **Cron (Linux/macOS)** and **Task Scheduler (Windows)** for **scheduled automation**.

# What's Next?

In **Chapter 19**, we will:

- Learn **how to automate web browsing and testing**.
- Use **Selenium and BeautifulSoup for web automation**.
- Automate **data extraction, form filling, and web scraping**.

# Chapter 19

# Cross-Platform Network Programming

Python is widely used for **network programming**, allowing developers to create **automated networking scripts, socket-based communication, and RESTful APIs** that work across **Windows, macOS, and Linux**.

This chapter explores:

1. **Using Python for network automation**
2. **Writing portable network scripts with sockets**
3. **Creating cross-platform RESTful APIs**

## 1. Using Python for Network Automation

Network automation helps **configure devices, monitor networks, and manage servers** without manual intervention. Python provides several libraries for **automating networking tasks**.

## 1.1 Automating Network Tasks with Paramiko (SSH)

Paramiko allows Python to **connect to remote devices** over SSH.

*Installing Paramiko*
bash

196

```
pip install paramiko
```
*Example: Running Commands on a Remote Server via SSH*
```
python

import paramiko

host = "192.168.1.10"
username = "admin"
password = "password"

client = paramiko.SSHClient()
client.set_missing_host_key_policy(paramiko.Aut
oAddPolicy())
client.connect(host,           username=username,
password=password)

stdin, stdout, stderr = client.exec_command("ls
-la")
print(stdout.read().decode())

client.close()
```

**Use Case:** Automating **remote server administration**.

---

# *1.2 Sending HTTP Requests with Requests Module*

Python's **requests** module simplifies **HTTP communication** with web services.

*Installing Requests*
```
bash

pip install requests
```

*Example: Checking Internet Connectivity*

python

```python
import requests

try:
    response                                    =
requests.get("https://www.google.com",
timeout=5)
    if response.status_code == 200:
        print("Internet is working!")
except requests.ConnectionError:
    print("No internet connection!")
```

 **Use Case:** Monitoring **network connectivity** in automated scripts.

---

# 2. Writing Portable Network Scripts with Sockets

Sockets allow Python programs to **communicate over a network** using **TCP or UDP protocols**.

## *2.1 Creating a Simple TCP Server*

python

```python
import socket

server        =        socket.socket(socket.AF_INET,
socket.SOCK_STREAM)
server.bind(("0.0.0.0", 9999))   # Bind to all
available interfaces on port 9999
server.listen(5)

print("Server listening on port 9999...")
```

```
while True:
    client, addr = server.accept()
    print(f"Connection from {addr}")
    client.send(b"Hello from Python server!\n")
    client.close()
```

# 2.2 Creating a Simple TCP Client

```python

import socket

client     =      socket.socket(socket.AF_INET,
socket.SOCK_STREAM)
client.connect(("127.0.0.1", 9999))

response = client.recv(1024)
print("Received:", response.decode())

client.close()
```

 **Use Case:** Creating **network communication scripts** for **IoT devices, remote commands, or chat applications**.

# 2.3 Broadcasting Messages with UDP

*UDP Server*
```python

import socket

server     =      socket.socket(socket.AF_INET,
socket.SOCK_DGRAM)
server.bind(("0.0.0.0", 8888))

print("UDP Server listening...")
```

199

```
while True:
    data, addr = server.recvfrom(1024)
    print(f"Received    '{data.decode()}'    from
{addr}")
```

*UDP Client*
python

```
import socket

client        =        socket.socket(socket.AF_INET,
socket.SOCK_DGRAM)
client.sendto(b"Hello        UDP        Server!",
("127.0.0.1", 8888))
client.close()
```

 **Use Case: Broadcasting messages** to multiple devices on a local network.

---

# 3. Creating Cross-Platform RESTful APIs

APIs allow applications to **communicate over a network** using **HTTP requests**.

## *3.1 Creating a Simple API with FastAPI*

*Installing FastAPI and Uvicorn*
bash

```
pip install fastapi uvicorn
```
*Creating app.py (FastAPI Server)*
python

```
from fastapi import FastAPI
```

```
app = FastAPI()

@app.get("/")
def home():
    return {"message": "Welcome to FastAPI!"}

@app.get("/info/{name}")
def info(name: str):
    return {"message": f"Hello, {name}!"}

if __name__ == "__main__":
    import uvicorn
    uvicorn.run(app, host="0.0.0.0", port=8000)
```

*Running the API Server*
```
bash

python app.py
```

### Test the API in a browser:

- http://127.0.0.1:8000/  →  {"message": "Welcome to FastAPI!"}
- http://127.0.0.1:8000/info/John  →  {"message": "Hello, John!"}

---

# 3.2 Consuming APIs with Python (REST Client)

```
python

import requests

response = requests.get("http://127.0.0.1:8000/info/Alice")
print(response.json())   # Output: {'message': 'Hello, Alice!'}
```

201

 **Use Case:** Connecting **Python applications to cloud services**.

## Conclusion

Python makes **cross-platform network programming easy**, from **automating network tasks** to **building APIs and socket-based applications**.

## *Key Takeaways:*

- **Use Paramiko** for **remote SSH automation**.
- **Use sockets** for **custom network communication**.
- **Use FastAPI** to build **cross-platform REST APIs**.

## What's Next?

In **Chapter 20**, we will:

- Learn **how to automate web browsing and testing**.
- Use **Selenium and BeautifulSoup for web automation**.
- Automate **data extraction, form filling, and web scraping**.

## Chapter 20

# Packaging Python Applications for Different Platforms

Python applications need to be **packaged and distributed** so that end users can run them **without installing Python or dependencies manually**. Packaging tools like **PyInstaller, cx_Freeze, and PyOxidizer** allow developers to create **executable files** for **Windows, macOS, and Linux**.

This chapter explores:

1. **Using PyInstaller, cx_Freeze, and PyOxidizer for packaging**
2. **Creating standalone executables for Windows, macOS, and Linux**
3. **Handling dependencies and versioning**

# 1. Using PyInstaller, cx_Freeze, and PyOxidizer for Packaging

Python does not natively compile into executables like C++ or Java, but **packaging tools** can bundle Python applications into **standalone executable files**.

## 1.1 PyInstaller: The Most Popular Packaging Tool

**Pros:**
Works on **Windows, macOS, and Linux.** Supports **one-file executables.** Compatible with **GUI and CLI applications.**

**Cons:**
Larger file sizes compared to compiled languages. Some antivirus software flags PyInstaller executables.

*Installing PyInstaller*
bash

```
pip install pyinstaller
```
*Packaging a Python Script (app.py) into an Executable*
bash

```
pyinstaller --onefile --windowed app.py
```

**Explanation:**

- **--onefile**: Packages everything into a **single executable.**
- **--windowed**: Hides the terminal window (for GUI apps).

**Windows Output:** `dist/app.exe`
**macOS/Linux Output:** `dist/app`

---

# *1.2 cx_Freeze: Alternative for Cross-Platform Packaging*

**Pros:**
Better support for **complex dependencies.**

Creates **smaller executables** than PyInstaller.
Works on **Windows, macOS, and Linux**.

**Cons:**
More configuration needed.
Slower than PyInstaller for simple projects.

*Installing cx_Freeze*
bash

```
pip install cx_Freeze
```
*Creating a setup.py for cx_Freeze*
python

```
from cx_Freeze import setup, Executable

setup(
    name="MyApp",
    version="1.0",
    description="A cross-platform Python app",
    executables=[Executable("app.py")]
)
```
*Building the Executable*
bash

```
python setup.py build
```

**Output:** Executables are stored in the `build/` directory.

# *1.3 PyOxidizer: Packaging Python into a Single Binary*

**Pros:**
Creates **smaller, faster executables** than PyInstaller.
Eliminates **dependency on Python interpreter**.

**Cons:**
More        difficult        to        configure.
Limited community support.

*Installing PyOxidizer*
```bash
bash
```

```
cargo install pyoxidizer
```
*Creating a Standalone Executable*
```bash
bash
```

```
pyoxidizer init-config
pyoxidizer build
```

**Best For:** High-performance applications that need **minimal runtime dependencies**.

---

# 2. Creating Executable Files for Windows, macOS, and Linux

Python applications need to be packaged differently for **each platform**.

| Platform | Tool | Command |
|---|---|---|
| **Windows (.exe)** | PyInstaller | `pyinstaller --onefile app.py` |
| **macOS (.app)** | PyInstaller | `pyinstaller --onefile --windowed app.py` |
| **Linux (binary)** | PyInstaller | `pyinstaller --onefile app.py` |

# *2.1 Packaging for Windows*

*Creating an Executable with PyInstaller*

bash

```
pyinstaller --onefile --windowed app.py
```

**Output:** dist/app.exe

*Creating an Installer for Windows*

Use **Inno Setup** to create an **installer**:

1. Install **Inno Setup** (Download).
2. Create a script (setup.iss):

   makefile

   ```
   [Setup]
   AppName=MyApp
   AppVersion=1.0
   DefaultDirName={pf}\MyApp
   OutputDir=.\dist
   OutputBaseFilename=MyAppInstaller
   [Files]
   Source: "dist\app.exe"; DestDir: "{app}"
   ```

3. Compile the script to generate an **installer .exe**.

---

# *2.2 Packaging for macOS*

*Creating a macOS Executable with PyInstaller*

bash

```
pyinstaller --onefile --windowed app.py
```

**Output:** dist/app

*Creating a macOS .app Bundle*

1. **Convert executable into an .app bundle:**

   bash

   ```
   pyinstaller --onefile --windowed --name
   "MyApp" app.py
   ```

2. **Notarizing and signing for macOS** (required for macOS security):

   bash

   ```
   codesign --deep --force --verbose --sign
   "Developer ID Application" dist/MyApp.app
   ```

**Use Case:** Distributing macOS applications via **dmg** or **App Store**.

---

# *2.3 Packaging for Linux*

*Creating a Standalone Linux Binary*
bash

```
pyinstaller --onefile app.py
```

**Output:** dist/app

*Creating a .deb Package for Ubuntu*
bash

```
dpkg-deb --build myapp_package
```

**Use Case:** Distributing Linux applications via **Debian-based package managers**.

---

# 3. Handling Dependencies and Versioning

A well-packaged Python application must **manage dependencies** efficiently.

## *3.1 Creating a `requirements.txt` File*

Ensure all dependencies are listed:

```bash

pip freeze > requirements.txt
```

## *3.2 Using Virtual Environments*

```bash

python -m venv myenv
source myenv/bin/activate  # macOS/Linux
myenv\Scripts\activate  # Windows
```

**Use Case:** Ensuring the app works across different Python versions.

---

## *3.3 Versioning with Semantic Versioning*

Follow the **Semantic Versioning (SemVer) standard**:

- **Major Version (x.0.0)** → Breaking changes.
- **Minor Version (0.x.0)** → New features, backward-compatible.
- **Patch Version (0.0.x)** → Bug fixes.

*Example: Setting a Version in* `setup.py`
```python
python

setup(
    name="MyApp",
    version="1.2.3",
    description="My cross-platform app",
)
```

**Use Case:** Keeping track of **feature updates and bug fixes**.

# Conclusion

Python's packaging tools **allow developers to distribute applications** as standalone executables across **Windows, macOS, and Linux**.

## *Key Takeaways:*

- **PyInstaller** → Best for **quick and easy packaging**.
- **cx_Freeze** → Great for **complex applications with dependencies**.
- **PyOxidizer** → Ideal for **minimal footprint applications**.
- **Versioning and dependencies** should be managed using **venvs and** `requirements.txt`.

# What's Next?

In **Chapter 21**, we will:

- Explore **deploying Python applications to cloud platforms**.
- Learn **how to host Python web applications on AWS, Heroku, and Google Cloud**.
- Understand **containerization with Docker for deployment**.

## Chapter 21

# Distributing Python Apps via PyPI, Snap, and Homebrew

Once a Python application is developed, it needs to be **distributed** so users can install and run it easily. This can be done via:

- **PyPI** (for Python libraries and command-line tools).
- **Snap and AppImage** (for cross-platform binary distribution).
- **Homebrew** (for macOS users).

This chapter explores:

1. **Publishing Python packages on PyPI**
2. **Creating Snap and AppImage distributions**
3. **Using Homebrew to distribute Python applications for macOS**

---

# 1. Publishing Python Packages on PyPI (Python Package Index)

PyPI (Python Package Index) is the official repository for **Python libraries and applications**. Users can install your package via `pip install yourpackage`.

## 1.1 Preparing the Package for PyPI

*1. Create a Directory and Add Your Package Code*
bash

```
mkdir mypackage
cd mypackage
```

# Create the package structure:

arduino

```
mypackage/
|—— mypackage/
|       |—— __init__.py
|       |—— mymodule.py
|—— setup.py
|—— README.md
|—— LICENSE
|—— requirements.txt
```

---

*2. Define setup.py for Packaging*

# Create a setup.py file to define package metadata:

python

```
from setuptools import setup, find_packages

setup(
    name="mypackage",
    version="1.0.0",
    author="Your Name",
    author_email="you@example.com",
    description="A sample Python package",
    long_description=open("README.md").read(),

long_description_content_type="text/markdown",

url="https://github.com/yourusername/mypackage"
,
    packages=find_packages(),
```

```
    install_requires=["requests"],        #    Add
dependencies
    classifiers=[
        "Programming Language :: Python :: 3",
        "License :: OSI Approved :: MIT License",
        "Operating System :: OS Independent",
    ],
    python_requires=">=3.6",
)
```

*3. Build the Package for PyPI*

Install twine and setuptools:

bash

pip install setuptools wheel twine

Then, generate the package:

bash

python setup.py sdist bdist_wheel

This creates a dist/ directory with the package files.

*4. Upload the Package to PyPI*

1. **Create a PyPI Account** at pypi.org.
2. **Upload the package**:

   bash

   twine upload dist/*

3. **Install and test your package**:

214

```
bash

pip install mypackage
```

**Use Case:** Distributing **Python libraries and CLI tools** globally.

# 2. Creating Snap and AppImage Distributions

For **cross-platform distribution**, Snap and AppImage allow users to install applications **without needing Python**.

## *2.1 Creating a Snap Package*

**Snap** is a universal package format that works on **Linux distributions like Ubuntu, Debian, and Fedora**.

*1. Install Snapcraft*
```
bash

sudo apt install snapcraft
```
*2. Create a snapcraft.yaml File*
```yaml
name: myapp
base: core20
version: "1.0"
summary: "A Python-based Snap application"
description: "My Python App as a Snap Package"
grade: stable
confinement: strict
```

```
apps:
  myapp:
    command: python3 $SNAP/bin/myscript.py

parts:
  myapp:
    plugin: python
    source: .
```

*3. Build and Publish the Snap Package*
```
bash
```

```
snapcraft
bash
```

```
snap install myapp.snap --dangerous   # Install
locally
bash
```

```
snapcraft push myapp.snap  # Upload to Snap Store
```

**Use Case:** Distributing **Python apps on Linux** without dependency issues.

---

# *2.2 Creating an AppImage*

**AppImage** is another **cross-platform** packaging format for **Linux**.

*1. Install AppImageTools*
```
bash
```

```
sudo apt install appimagetool
```
*2. Create the AppImage Package*

1. **Create a folder with your app**:

   ```
   bash
   ```

216

```
mkdir -p MyApp.AppDir/usr/bin
cp myscript.py MyApp.AppDir/usr/bin/
chmod +x MyApp.AppDir/usr/bin/myscript.py
```

2. **Add an AppRun script**:

```
bash
```

```
echo    -e    '#!/bin/bash\nexec    python3
/usr/bin/myscript.py'                          >
MyApp.AppDir/AppRun
chmod +x MyApp.AppDir/AppRun
```

3. **Generate the AppImage**:

```
bash
```

```
appimagetool MyApp.AppDir
```

**Use Case:** Distributing **standalone applications for Linux**.

---

# 3. Creating a Homebrew Formula for macOS

Homebrew is a **package manager for macOS** that allows users to install software via:

```
bash
```

```
brew install myapp
```

---

# *3.1 Creating a Homebrew Formula*

217

*1. Write a Homebrew Formula (`myapp.rb`)*
```ruby
ruby

class Myapp < Formula
  desc "My Python-based Homebrew package"
  homepage
"https://github.com/yourusername/myapp"
  url
"https://github.com/yourusername/myapp/archive/
v1.0.tar.gz"
  sha256 "your_tarball_sha256_checksum"

  depends_on "python"

  def install
    bin.install "myscript.py"
  end

  test do
    system "#{bin}/myscript.py", "--version"
  end
end
```

*2. Publish to a Homebrew Tap*

1. **Fork the Homebrew repository** on GitHub.
2. **Create a `homebrew-myrepo` repository**.
3. **Upload `myapp.rb`** to the repository.

*3. Install Your Homebrew Package*
```bash
bash

brew tap yourusername/myrepo
brew install myapp
```

**Use Case:** Distributing **command-line tools for macOS users.**

# Conclusion

Python applications can be distributed across **multiple platforms** using **PyPI, Snap, AppImage, and Homebrew**.

## *Key Takeaways:*

- **PyPI** is best for **Python packages and libraries**.
- **Snap** is great for **Linux package distribution**.
- **AppImage** creates **standalone Linux applications**.
- **Homebrew** allows **easy installation on macOS**.

# What's Next?

In **Chapter 22**, we will:

- Learn **how to publish Python applications as Docker containers**.
- Use **Docker to containerize Python applications for deployment**.
- Deploy applications using **Docker Compose and Kubernetes**.

## *Chapter 22*

# *Cross-Platform Mobile Deployment*

Python is not typically used for mobile app development, but frameworks like **BeeWare** and **Kivy** allow developers to create and deploy **cross-platform mobile applications**. This chapter covers:

1. **Using BeeWare and Kivy for mobile packaging**
2. **Deploying Python apps on Android (APK) and iOS (IPA)**
3. **Challenges of mobile compatibility**

---

# 1. Using BeeWare and Kivy for Mobile Packaging

Python applications can be **compiled and packaged** for Android and iOS using two main frameworks:

| Feature | BeeWare | Kivy |
|---|---|---|
| Language | Uses **native UI elements** | Uses **OpenGL-based UI** |
| Ease of Use | Easier (Python + native widgets) | More control, but harder to set up |
| Performance | Fast (native components) | Slower (renders everything manually) |

| Feature | BeeWare | Kivy |
|---|---|---|
| Supported Platforms | Android, iOS, macOS, Windows, Linux | Android, iOS, Windows, macOS, Linux |

# 1.1 Setting Up BeeWare for Mobile Development

**BeeWare** allows developers to create **native mobile applications** with a Python backend.

*1. Install Briefcase (BeeWare's Packaging Tool)*
```bash
```

```
pip install briefcase
```
*2. Create a New BeeWare App*
```bash
```

```
briefcase new
```

This generates a project structure for a **mobile-ready application**.

*3. Run the App on Desktop*
```bash
```

```
briefcase dev
```

# 1.2 Setting Up Kivy for Mobile Development

Kivy provides **OpenGL-based graphics and multi-touch support**, making it ideal for **games and custom UI apps**.

*1. Install Kivy*
bash

```
pip install kivy
```
*2. Create a Basic Kivy App*
python

```
from kivy.app import App
from kivy.uix.label import Label

class MyApp(App):
    def build(self):
        return     Label(text="Hello,     Mobile
World!")

MyApp().run()
```

 **Use Case:** Kivy is ideal for **games, multimedia, and custom UIs**.

---

# 2. Deploying Python Apps on Android (APK) and iOS (IPA)

## *2.1 Deploying a BeeWare App on Android*

*1. Install Android SDK and Dependencies*
bash

```
briefcase create android
```

222

*2. Build the Android App*
bash

```
briefcase build android
```
*3. Package the Android App (APK)*
bash

```
briefcase package android
```

**Output:** dist/app.apk

---

# *2.2 Deploying a Kivy App on Android*

Kivy uses **Buildozer** to generate APK files.

*1. Install Buildozer*
bash

```
pip install buildozer
```
*2. Initialize a Buildozer Project*
bash

```
buildozer init
```

This creates a buildozer.spec configuration file.

*3. Edit buildozer.spec File*

- **Set package name:**

  ini

  ```
  package.name = MyKivyApp
  ```

- **Enable Android packaging:**

223

```
ini

android.api = 30
```
*4. Build the APK File*
```
bash

buildozer -v android debug
```

**Output:** bin/MyKivyApp.apk

---

# 2.3 Deploying a Python App on iOS

Both **BeeWare and Kivy** support iOS, but **macOS and Xcode are required** for iOS builds.

*1. Install Required Tools*
```
bash

pip install briefcase
```
*2. Build the App for iOS*
```
bash

briefcase create iOS
briefcase build iOS
```
*3. Package as an .ipa File*
```
bash

briefcase package iOS
```

**Output:** dist/MyApp.ipa (ready for the App Store).

---

224

# 3. Challenges of Mobile Compatibility

Python was **not originally designed for mobile applications**, leading to **challenges** like:

# *3.1 Performance Issues*

- Python apps are **slower than native apps** (Objective-C, Swift, Java).
- Solution: **Use native libraries** where possible.

# *3.2 App Store Restrictions*

- Apple's App Store **does not allow JIT compilation**, affecting Kivy.
- Solution: **Use BeeWare for iOS apps** (it compiles to native code).

# *3.3 Large File Sizes*

- Python-based APKs are **larger** than native apps.
- Solution: **Use PyOxidizer** to package dependencies efficiently.

# Conclusion

Python-based mobile apps **can be built and deployed** using **BeeWare and Kivy**, but they come with **performance and compatibility trade-offs**.

 **Key Takeaways:**

- **BeeWare is best** for **native UI apps**.
- **Kivy is ideal** for **custom UIs and games**.
- **Buildozer (Kivy) and Briefcase (BeeWare)** help create **Android APKs and iOS IPAs**.
- **Performance limitations** exist but can be optimized.

# What's Next?

In **Chapter 23**, we will:

- **Optimize Python applications for cross-platform performance**.
- **Use Just-In-Time (JIT) compilation** to speed up execution.
- **Reduce application memory usage and improve efficiency**.

## *Chapter 23*

# *Optimizing Performance in Cross-Platform Python Applications*

Python is a **powerful but interpreted language**, which can lead to **performance bottlenecks** in cross-platform applications. To ensure smooth performance across **Windows, macOS, and Linux**, developers must **profile, optimize, and reduce memory usage**.

This chapter explores:

1. **Profiling and performance testing tools**
2. **Using Cython, Numba, and PyPy for speed improvements**
3. **Reducing memory usage and improving efficiency**

---

# 1. Profiling and Performance Testing Tools

Before optimizing, it's important to **identify performance bottlenecks**. Python provides several profiling tools:

| Tool | Use Case |
|---|---|
| cProfile | **Built-in Python profiler** for function performance |
| timeit | Measure **execution time of small code snippets** |

| Tool | Use Case |
|------|----------|
| `line_profiler` | **Line-by-line performance analysis** |
| `memory_profiler` | Detect **memory usage issues** |
| `Py-Spy` | **Real-time CPU profiling** (low overhead) |

# 1.1 Using `cProfile` for Function Performance

```python
import cProfile

def slow_function():
    total = 0
    for i in range(10**6):
        total += i
    return total

cProfile.run("slow_function()")
```

**Use Case:** Finding **slow functions in large applications**.

# 1.2 Measuring Execution Time with `timeit`

```python
import timeit

def test_function():
```

```
    return sum(range(10**6))
```

```
execution_time = timeit.timeit(test_function,
number=10)
print(f"Execution time: {execution_time:.5f}
seconds")
```

 **Use Case: Comparing the efficiency** of different algorithms.

## *1.3 Detecting High Memory Usage with* `memory_profiler`

```python

from memory_profiler import profile

@profile
def create_large_list():
    return [i for i in range(10**7)]

create_large_list()
```

 **Use Case:** Identifying **functions that consume excessive memory**.

# 2. Using Cython, Numba, and PyPy for Speed Improvements

Python's **dynamic typing and interpreted execution** make it **slower** than compiled languages. **Cython, Numba, and PyPy** help improve speed significantly.

# 2.1 Compiling Python Code with Cython

**Cython** converts Python code into **C extensions**, making it **much faster**.

*1. Install Cython*
bash

```
pip install cython
```

*2. Convert Python to Cython (`fast.pyx`)*
cython

```
def add(int a, int b):
    return a + b
```

*3. Compile the Cython Code*

Create a `setup.py` file:

python

```
from setuptools import setup
from Cython.Build import cythonize

setup(
    ext_modules=cythonize("fast.pyx")
)
```

Run the build:

bash

```
python setup.py build_ext --inplace
```

 **Use Case: Converting slow Python functions to compiled C code**.

---

# *2.2 Accelerating Code with Numba (JIT Compilation)*

**Numba** speeds up Python by **compiling functions at runtime**.

*1. Install Numba*
```
bash

pip install numba
```
*2. Apply JIT Compilation*
```python
python

from numba import jit

@jit(nopython=True)
def fast_function():
    total = 0
    for i in range(10**6):
        total += i
    return total

print(fast_function())
```

 **Use Case: Accelerating loops and numerical operations**.

---

# *2.3 Running Python on PyPy (A Faster Interpreter)*

**PyPy** is a **Just-In-Time (JIT) compiled version of Python** that improves performance.

*1. Install PyPy*
bash

```
sudo apt install pypy3   # Linux/macOS
```
*2. Run a Script with PyPy*
bash

```
pypy3 myscript.py
```

 **Use Case: Speeding up existing Python applications without modifying code**.

---

# 3. Reducing Memory Usage and Improving Efficiency

Memory optimization ensures **Python applications use resources efficiently** across platforms.

---

# *3.1 Using Generators Instead of Lists*

Generators **reduce memory usage** compared to lists.

*Inefficient (Consumes More Memory)*
python

```
nums = [i for i in range(10**7)]
```
*Optimized (Uses Generators Instead)*
python

```
nums = (i for i in range(10**7))
```

**Use Case: Handling large datasets efficiently**.

# 3.2 Using slots to Reduce Object Memory Usage

Python objects use **more memory than necessary** due to dynamic attribute storage.

*Without slots (More Memory Usage)*
```
python

class MyClass:
    def __init__(self, name, age):
        self.name = name
        self.age = age
```
*With slots (Less Memory Usage)*
```
python

class MyClass:
    __slots__ = ["name", "age"]
    def __init__(self, name, age):
        self.name = name
        self.age = age
```

**Use Case: Optimizing object-heavy applications**.

# 3.3 Using array Instead of Lists for Numeric Data

Python lists **consume more memory** than necessary for numeric data.

*Inefficient List Usage*
```
python
```

```
numbers = [1, 2, 3, 4, 5]  # Takes more memory
```
*Optimized with array*
```
python
```

```
import array
numbers = array.array("i", [1, 2, 3, 4, 5])  #
More memory-efficient
```

**Use Case: Optimizing numerical data storage**.

# Conclusion

Python applications **can be optimized for speed and memory efficiency** using the right techniques.

## *Key Takeaways:*

- Use **profiling tools** (`cProfile`, `timeit`, `memory_profiler`) to find bottlenecks.
- Use **Cython or Numba** to speed up computation-heavy functions.
- Use **PyPy** for a performance boost **without modifying code**.
- Optimize memory with **generators, `slots`, and `array`**.

# What's Next?

In **Chapter 24**, we will:

- **Secure Python applications** against **common vulnerabilities**.
- **Use cryptography** for **data encryption**.
- **Harden APIs** to **prevent security breaches**.

# Chapter 24

# *Ensuring Security in Cross-Platform Applications*

Security is a critical concern when developing **cross-platform Python applications**. Whether it's a **desktop, mobile, or web application**, securing data, authentication, and user interactions is essential.

This chapter explores:

1. **Best practices for securing Python applications**
2. **Handling user authentication securely**
3. **Protecting against common vulnerabilities (SQL injection, XSS, CSRF)**

---

# 1. Best Practices for Securing Python Applications

Every **Python application** should follow security best practices to **protect user data and prevent attacks**.

## *1.1 Keep Dependencies Updated*

Regularly update **third-party libraries** to **patch security vulnerabilities**.

*Check Outdated Packages*
bash

```
pip list --outdated
```
*Upgrade Packages*
```
bash

pip install --upgrade <package_name>
```

**Use Case: Preventing exploits in outdated dependencies**.

# *1.2 Securely Store API Keys and Credentials*

**Never hardcode credentials** inside Python scripts. Instead, use **environment variables**.

*Using Environment Variables for Secure Storage*
```
python

import os

db_password = os.getenv("DATABASE_PASSWORD")
```

 **Use Case: Keeping sensitive information out of source code**.

# *1.3 Use HTTPS Instead of HTTP*

Whenever making **network requests**, ensure **HTTPS** is enforced.

*Secure API Requests with HTTPS*
```
python
```

```
import requests

response      =      requests.get("https://secure-
api.com/data")
```

**Use Case: Preventing data interception (Man-in-the-Middle attacks).**

---

# 2. Handling User Authentication Securely

Authentication is a **prime target for attackers**. It must be **secure, encrypted, and resistant to brute-force attacks**.

---

## *2.1 Hashing Passwords Securely*

Never store passwords as plain text—**always hash and salt them**.

*Using bcrypt to Hash Passwords*
```
bash

pip install bcrypt
python

import bcrypt

password = "user_password".encode()
salt = bcrypt.gensalt()
hashed_password = bcrypt.hashpw(password, salt)

print(hashed_password)
```

Use Case: **Preventing password leaks in case of a data breach**.

---

# 2.2 Implementing Secure User Login

*Checking Passwords Against Hashed Values*

python

```
def verify_password(stored_hash, user_password):
    return
bcrypt.checkpw(user_password.encode(),
stored_hash)
```

Use Case: **Preventing attackers from accessing accounts with leaked passwords**.

---

# 2.3 Using JSON Web Tokens (JWT) for Authentication

JWT is widely used for **secure authentication in web and mobile applications**.

*Installing PyJWT*

bash

```
pip install pyjwt
```

*Generating a JWT Token*

python

```
import jwt
import datetime
```

```
SECRET_KEY = "secure_key"

def generate_jwt(user_id):
    payload   =  {"user_id":   user_id,   "exp":
datetime.datetime.utcnow()                       +
datetime.timedelta(hours=1)}
    return    jwt.encode(payload,    SECRET_KEY,
algorithm="HS256")

token = generate_jwt(123)
print(token)
```

**Use Case: Token-based authentication for APIs and mobile apps**.

---

## 2.4 Validating JWT Tokens

```python
def verify_jwt(token):
    try:
        decoded_token    =    jwt.decode(token,
SECRET_KEY, algorithms=["HS256"])
        return decoded_token
    except jwt.ExpiredSignatureError:
        return "Token expired"
    except jwt.InvalidTokenError:
        return "Invalid token"
```

**Use Case: Ensuring users cannot manipulate JWT tokens**.

---

# 3. Protecting Against Common Vulnerabilities

Cross-platform applications must **be hardened** against common **security threats**.

## *3.1 Preventing SQL Injection*

An attacker can exploit **poorly handled SQL queries** to **steal or modify database data**.

*Unsafe Query (Vulnerable to SQL Injection)*
```python
cursor.execute(f"SELECT * FROM users WHERE username = '{username}'")
```
*Safe Query (Using Parameterized Queries)*
```python
cursor.execute("SELECT * FROM users WHERE username = ?", (username,))
```

 **Use Case: Preventing attackers from modifying SQL queries**.

## *3.2 Preventing Cross-Site Scripting (XSS)*

XSS allows attackers to **inject malicious JavaScript** into web applications.

*Unsafe Code (Vulnerable to XSS)*
python

```
@app.route("/search")
def search():
    query = request.args.get("q")
    return      f"<h1>Search      results      for:
{query}</h1>"
```

*Safe Code (Escaping User Input)*
python

```
from flask import escape

@app.route("/search")
def search():
    query = escape(request.args.get("q"))
    return      f"<h1>Search      results      for:
{query}</h1>"
```

 **Use Case: Preventing attackers from injecting malicious scripts**.

---

# 3.3 Preventing Cross-Site Request Forgery (CSRF)

CSRF tricks users into **performing unwanted actions** on authenticated websites.

*Solution: Use CSRF Tokens*
bash

```
pip install flask-wtf
```
python

242

```
from flask_wtf.csrf import CSRFProtect

app = Flask(__name__)
csrf = CSRFProtect(app)
```

**Use Case: Preventing attackers from forcing users to execute unwanted actions**.

# 3.4 Limiting Login Attempts (Brute Force Protection)

Attackers can try **millions of password combinations** to break into accounts.

*Solution: Rate-Limit Login Attempts*
```
bash

pip install flask-limiter
python

from flask import Flask
from flask_limiter import Limiter

app = Flask(__name__)
limiter    =    Limiter(app,    key_func=lambda:
request.remote_addr)

@app.route("/login", methods=["POST"])
@limiter.limit("5 per minute")
def login():
    return "Login request received!"
```

**Use Case: Preventing brute-force login attacks**.

# Conclusion

Security is **essential** for cross-platform applications. Implementing best practices **reduces risks and ensures safe user experiences**.

## *Key Takeaways:*

- Use bcrypt for **password hashing**.
- Use **JWT for secure authentication**.
- Prevent **SQL injection** with **parameterized queries**.
- **Escape user input** to prevent **XSS attacks**.
- Use **CSRF tokens** to protect against **unauthorized actions**.
- **Rate-limit login attempts** to prevent **brute-force attacks**.

# What's Next?

In **Chapter 25**, we will:

- **Deploy Python applications securely** in production environments.
- **Use Docker and Kubernetes** for **isolated deployments**.
- **Set up HTTPS, firewalls, and API security measures**.

# Chapter 25

# The Role of AI and Machine Learning in Cross-Platform Applications

Artificial Intelligence (AI) and Machine Learning (ML) are revolutionizing **cross-platform applications**, enabling intelligent features like **image recognition, chatbots, predictive analytics, and automation**. Python, being the dominant language for AI, offers several powerful frameworks like **TensorFlow, PyTorch, and Scikit-learn** for integrating AI models into applications.

This chapter explores:

1. **Integrating AI models into Python applications**
2. **Using TensorFlow, PyTorch, and Scikit-learn for ML development**
3. **Deploying AI-powered applications on multiple platforms**

# 1. Integrating AI Models into Python Applications

AI can enhance **cross-platform applications** by:

- **Automating decision-making** (e.g., fraud detection, recommendation engines).
- **Enhancing user experience** (e.g., voice assistants, personalized suggestions).

- **Improving security** (e.g., AI-powered authentication, anomaly detection).

# *1.1 Installing AI/ML Frameworks in Python*

To get started with AI development, install the necessary libraries:

bash

```
pip install tensorflow torch torchvision scikit-
learn
```

**Use Case:** Running **deep learning and machine learning models** in Python applications.

# *1.2 Loading and Using Pre-trained AI Models*

Instead of training models from scratch, we can **use pre-trained models**.

*Example: Using OpenAI's GPT for Text Generation*
python

```
from transformers import pipeline

generator      =      pipeline("text-generation",
model="gpt2")
```

```
response = generator("AI is transforming cross-
platform applications", max_length=50)
print(response)
```

**Use Case: Adding AI-generated text features to Python apps.**

# *1.3 Running an AI Model in a Flask Web App*

```bash
pip install flask tensorflow
python
```

```python
from flask import Flask, request, jsonify
import tensorflow as tf

app = Flask(__name__)
model                                        =
tf.keras.models.load_model("my_model.h5")    #
Load a trained AI model

@app.route("/predict", methods=["POST"])
def predict():
    data = request.json["input"]
    prediction = model.predict([data])
    return            jsonify({"prediction":
prediction.tolist()})

if __name__ == "__main__":
    app.run(debug=True)
```

**Use Case: Deploying AI models as APIs for integration into web apps.**

# 2. Using TensorFlow, PyTorch, and Scikit-learn for ML Development

## *2.1 Training a Simple Machine Learning Model with Scikit-learn*

Scikit-learn is used for **traditional machine learning models**.

```python
python

from      sklearn.model_selection      import
train_test_split
from          sklearn.ensemble         import
RandomForestClassifier
from sklearn.datasets import load_iris

# Load dataset
iris = load_iris()
X_train,    X_test,    y_train,    y_test    =
train_test_split(iris.data,       iris.target,
test_size=0.2)

# Train model
model = RandomForestClassifier()
model.fit(X_train, y_train)

# Make predictions
print(model.predict(X_test))
```

 **Use Case: Adding AI-powered predictions to Python applications**.

## 2.2 Training a Deep Learning Model with TensorFlow

TensorFlow is used for **deep learning and neural networks**.

```python
import tensorflow as tf
from tensorflow import keras
import numpy as np

# Generate dummy data
X = np.random.rand(100, 10)
y = np.random.randint(2, size=(100, 1))

# Define model
model = keras.Sequential([
    keras.layers.Dense(32, activation="relu"),
    keras.layers.Dense(1, activation="sigmoid")
])

# Compile and train model
model.compile(optimizer="adam",
loss="binary_crossentropy",
metrics=["accuracy"])
model.fit(X, y, epochs=10)

# Save model
model.save("ai_model.h5")
```

 **Use Case: Building deep learning applications like image recognition and NLP**.

## 2.3 Using PyTorch for Advanced AI Models

PyTorch is popular for **research-based AI and flexible neural networks**.

```python
import torch
import torch.nn as nn
import torch.optim as optim

# Define a simple model
class NeuralNet(nn.Module):
    def __init__(self):
        super(NeuralNet, self).__init__()
        self.fc1 = nn.Linear(10, 32)
        self.fc2 = nn.Linear(32, 1)

    def forward(self, x):
        x = torch.relu(self.fc1(x))
        return torch.sigmoid(self.fc2(x))

# Train model
model = NeuralNet()
criterion = nn.BCELoss()
optimizer = optim.Adam(model.parameters())

# Dummy data
X = torch.rand(100, 10)
y = torch.randint(0, 2, (100, 1)).float()

# Training loop
for epoch in range(10):
    optimizer.zero_grad()
    output = model(X)
    loss = criterion(output, y)
    loss.backward()
    optimizer.step()

print("Model trained successfully")
```

**Use Case: Deploying PyTorch models in AI-powered applications**.

# 3. Deploying AI-Powered Applications on Multiple Platforms

## *3.1 Deploying an AI Model as a REST API*

Deploying AI models as an API **allows them to be integrated into mobile, web, and desktop applications**.

*Steps to Deploy AI Model as an API*

1. Train the AI model using TensorFlow, PyTorch, or Scikit-learn.
2. Save the trained model (`model.h5` or `model.pth`).
3. Create a REST API using **Flask or FastAPI**.
4. Deploy the API to **cloud services (AWS, Google Cloud, Azure)**.

**Use Case: Making AI models available for multiple platforms**.

## *3.2 Deploying AI Models on Mobile with Kivy and BeeWare*

**Kivy & BeeWare** allow AI models to be used in **mobile applications**.

251

*Using TensorFlow in a Mobile App*
python

```
import tensorflow as tf

model                                    =
tf.keras.models.load_model("ai_model.h5")
prediction = model.predict([[0.1, 0.2, 0.3, 0.4,
0.5]])
print(prediction)
```

**Use Case: Adding AI-powered features to mobile applications**.

# *3.3 Deploying AI Models on Edge Devices*

AI models can also be deployed on **edge devices like Raspberry Pi, NVIDIA Jetson, and IoT devices**.

*Optimizing AI Models for Edge Devices*
bash

```
pip install tflite_runtime
python

import tflite_runtime.interpreter as tflite

interpreter                              =
tflite.Interpreter(model_path="model.tflite")
interpreter.allocate_tensors()
```

**Use Case: Running AI models efficiently on low-power devices**.

# Conclusion

Python's AI frameworks enable **cross-platform applications** to be **intelligent, predictive, and automated**.

## *Key Takeaways:*

- **TensorFlow & PyTorch** power **deep learning applications**.
- **Scikit-learn** provides **machine learning models for predictive analytics**.
- **AI models can be deployed as APIs** for cross-platform use.
- **Mobile and Edge AI applications** are possible with **Kivy, BeeWare, and TensorFlow Lite**.

## What's Next?

In **Chapter 26**, we will:

- Explore **future trends in cross-platform development**.
- Learn **how AI, cloud computing, and 5G** will shape the future.
- Discover **new frameworks that simplify Python development**.

# Chapter 26

# Emerging Trends in Cross-Platform Development

Cross-platform development is **evolving rapidly**, with new technologies like **serverless computing, WebAssembly (Wasm), and Rust integration** reshaping how applications are built and deployed. Python remains at the forefront of these changes, adapting to **new paradigms and performance optimizations**.

This chapter explores:

1. **The rise of serverless computing**
2. **The impact of WebAssembly (Wasm) and Rust integration**
3. **The future of multi-platform programming**

---

# 1. The Rise of Serverless Computing

Serverless computing is transforming **how applications are deployed and scaled**, eliminating the need for managing servers while improving **cost efficiency and scalability**.

## 1.1 What is Serverless Computing?

Serverless computing allows applications to run **on-demand in the cloud** without needing **traditional infrastructure management**.

| Feature | Traditional Servers | Serverless Computing |
|---|---|---|
| Infrastructure | Managed by developers | Managed by cloud provider |
| Scaling | Manual scaling required | Auto-scales dynamically |
| Cost | Pay for uptime | Pay only when the app runs |

**Use Case: Deploying Python APIs, data processing jobs, and event-driven applications**.

# 1.2 Deploying a Serverless Python Function on AWS Lambda

AWS Lambda is a leading **serverless platform** that runs Python functions **on demand**.

*1. Install AWS CLI and Boto3*
bash

```
pip install boto3
```
*2. Create a Python Lambda Function (`lambda_function.py`)*
python

```
import json

def lambda_handler(event, context):
    return {
        "statusCode": 200,
        "body":  json.dumps("Hello    from    AWS
Lambda!")
```

255

}

*3. Deploy the Function to AWS*

bash

```
aws   lambda   create-function   --function-name
myLambdaFunction   --runtime   python3.9   --role
myIAMRole                              --handler
lambda_function.lambda_handler      --zip-file
fileb://function.zip
```

**Use Case: Building auto-scaling backend services without managing servers**.

---

# *1.3 Serverless Python Frameworks: FastAPI + AWS Lambda*

FastAPI can be deployed in a **serverless environment** using **AWS Lambda**.

*Deploying FastAPI on AWS Lambda*

bash

```
pip install mangum
python

from fastapi import FastAPI
from mangum import Mangum

app = FastAPI()

@app.get("/")
def home():
    return   {"message":   "FastAPI   running
serverless!"}

handler = Mangum(app)
```

**Use Case: Scalable APIs that run only when needed**.

## 2. The Impact of WebAssembly (Wasm) and Rust Integration

WebAssembly (Wasm) is **changing how Python applications run in the browser**, making them **faster and more portable**.

## *2.1 What is WebAssembly (Wasm)?*

WebAssembly is a **binary instruction format** that runs Python **inside web browsers**, providing:

- **Near-native speed** performance.
- **Secure execution** in sandboxed environments.
- **Cross-platform compatibility** (Windows, macOS, Linux, Web).

 **Use Case: Running Python code in the browser without requiring a Python runtime**.

## *2.2 Running Python in WebAssembly Using Pyodide*

Pyodide compiles **Python to WebAssembly,** allowing it to **run in the browser**.

*1. Install Pyodide*
bash

```
pip install pyodide
```
*2. Run Python Code in the Browser*
html

```
<script type="pyodide">
    import math
    print(math.sqrt(25))
</script>
```

**Use Case: Bringing Python-powered applications to the web with zero installation**.

---

# *2.3 Rust + Python for High-Performance Cross-Platform Apps*

Rust is **fast, memory-safe, and cross-platform**, making it an excellent companion for Python.

| Feature | Python | Rust |
|---|---|---|
| **Performance** | Slower (interpreted) | Fast (compiled) |
| **Memory Safety** | Uses garbage collection | Memory-safe without garbage collection |
| **Best For** | AI, scripting, automation | High-performance systems, WebAssembly |

258

**Use Case: Combining Python's flexibility with Rust's speed for AI, automation, and web apps**.

# *2.4 Integrating Rust with Python (PyO3)*

PyO3 allows Rust functions to be **called directly from Python**.

*1. Install PyO3*

bash

```
pip install maturin
```

*2. Create a Rust Function (lib.rs)*

rust

```
use pyo3::prelude::*;

#[pyfunction]
fn add(a: i32, b: i32) -> i32 {
    a + b
}

#[pymodule]
fn rust_math(py: Python, m: &PyModule) ->
PyResult<()> {
    m.add_function(wrap_pyfunction!(add, m)?)?;
    Ok(())
}
```

*3. Compile and Use in Python*

python

```
import rust_math
print(rust_math.add(3, 5))
```

**Use Case: Speeding up Python applications with Rust for performance-critical tasks.**

# 3. The Future of Multi-Platform Programming

The future of **cross-platform Python development** is shaped by **new technologies and best practices.**

## *3.1 The Shift Towards Multi-Cloud and Edge Computing*

- **Applications will run across multiple cloud providers** (AWS, Azure, Google Cloud).
- **Edge computing** will reduce latency for real-time applications.
- **Python will integrate deeper with IoT devices and AI on the edge**.

**Use Case: Running AI models on mobile, IoT, and cloud seamlessly.**

## *3.2 Python's Role in the Future of Cross-Platform Development*

Python will continue to dominate **cross-platform development** by integrating with:

- **WebAssembly (for browser-based execution).**
- **Rust (for high-performance computing).**
- **Serverless (for auto-scaling applications).**
- **AI and automation (for intelligent cross-platform applications).**

**Use Case: Building a single Python application that runs on mobile, desktop, web, and cloud.**

# 3.3 Unified Tooling for Cross-Platform Development

Emerging frameworks are simplifying **Python's cross-platform capabilities**:

- **Pyodide** → Python in the browser.
- **BeeWare** → Python for native UI apps.
- **Rust + Python** → High-performance applications.
- **Serverless FastAPI** → Scalable cloud services.

**Use Case: One Python codebase running on all platforms.**

# Conclusion

Python's future in **cross-platform development** is driven by:

261

- Serverless computing for scalable applications.
- WebAssembly for browser-based Python execution.
- Rust integration for high-performance workloads.

## *Key Takeaways:*

- Serverless computing enables scalable, cost-efficient Python apps.
- WebAssembly (Pyodide) brings Python to the browser.
- Rust and Python (PyO3) combine performance and flexibility.
- Future applications will be cloud-native, cross-device, and AI-powered.

---

## What's Next?

This concludes the **final chapter** of *The Complete Guide to Cross-Platform Programming in Python*.

In the future:

- Python will integrate more with cloud and AI.
- WebAssembly and Rust will enhance Python's capabilities.
- Cross-platform development will become more seamless and efficient.

**Your journey in Python cross-platform development is just beginning!**

## Chapter 27

# *Final Thoughts: Best Practices for Long-Term Cross-Platform Success*

Successfully developing and maintaining **cross-platform Python applications** requires **strategic planning, the right tools, and continuous adaptation** to emerging technologies. This final chapter provides best practices for **ensuring long-term success** in cross-platform development.

This chapter explores:

1. Choosing the right tools for your projects
2. Keeping up with cross-platform development trends
3. Scaling applications effectively across different ecosystems

---

# 1. Choosing the Right Tools for Your Projects

Every project is unique, and selecting the right **frameworks, databases, and deployment strategies** is critical for long-term maintainability.

---

# *1.1 Selecting the Best Python Framework for Your Application*

| Application Type | Recommended Frameworks |
|---|---|
| Desktop GUI | Tkinter, PyQt, Kivy, BeeWare |
| Web Applications | Django, FastAPI, Flask |
| Mobile Development | Kivy, BeeWare |
| Machine Learning & AI | TensorFlow, PyTorch, Scikit-learn |
| Game Development | Pygame, Panda3D, Godot (with Python) |
| Automation & Scripting | Selenium, PyAutoGUI, Fabric |
| Cloud Services & APIs | AWS Lambda (Serverless), FastAPI, Flask |
| Embedded & IoT | MicroPython, CircuitPython, Raspberry Pi |

**Best Practice: Choose a framework that aligns with your application's needs, scalability, and platform requirements**.

# 1.2 Choosing the Right Database for Cross-Platform Applications

Databases must be chosen based on **performance, scalability, and cross-platform support**.

| Database | Best Use Case |
|---|---|
| **SQLite** | Local storage, lightweight applications |
| **PostgreSQL** | Scalable, enterprise-grade applications |
| **MongoDB** | Flexible, NoSQL, real-time apps |
| **Firebase** | Cloud-based, mobile-friendly data storage |
| **DynamoDB** | Serverless applications |

**Best Practice: For cloud-based applications, choose a scalable database that integrates with Python ORM frameworks (SQLAlchemy, Pydantic, etc.).**

# *1.3 Packaging and Deployment Strategies*

| Platform | Packaging Tool |
|---|---|
| **Windows (.exe)** | PyInstaller, cx_Freeze |
| **macOS (.app)** | PyInstaller, Homebrew |
| **Linux (.deb/.rpm)** | Snap, AppImage, Docker |
| **Web (Browser-Based)** | Pyodide (WebAssembly) |
| **Mobile (Android/iOS)** | Kivy (Buildozer), BeeWare (Briefcase) |

**Best Practice: Use platform-native packaging tools to ensure smooth deployment and a better user experience**.

---

# 2. Keeping Up with Cross-Platform Development Trends

Technology evolves rapidly, and staying ahead is essential for long-term success.

---

# *2.1 Following Industry Trends in Cross-Platform Development*

**Current trends shaping cross-platform development:**

- **Serverless Computing** – Run Python apps without managing servers (AWS Lambda, Google Cloud Functions).
- **WebAssembly (Wasm)** – Running Python in the browser via **Pyodide and WasmEdge**.
- **Python + Rust Integration** – Using **Rust for performance-critical Python components**.
- **Edge Computing** – Deploying AI and analytics on **IoT and edge devices**.
- **AI and ML Integration** – Embedding **AI models in cross-platform apps** for automation and personalization.

**Best Practice: Regularly explore new frameworks and technologies to ensure your applications stay competitive**.

266

# *2.2 Learning from the Open-Source Community*

Python's strength comes from its **vibrant open-source ecosystem**.

**How to stay updated:**

- **Follow Python Core Development** (Python.org)
- **Read Industry Blogs & Forums** (Real Python, r/Python on Reddit)
- **Attend Conferences** (PyCon, EuroPython, PyData)
- **Contribute to Open-Source Projects** (GitHub, OpenAI, NumPy)

 **Best Practice: Engaging with the open-source community provides insights into future developments and best practices**.

# 3. Scaling Applications Effectively Across Different Ecosystems

Scaling Python applications involves **optimizing performance, managing infrastructure, and handling growth**.

# 3.1 Optimizing Performance for Scalable Cross-Platform Applications

| Optimization Area | Best Practice |
| --- | --- |
| Execution Speed | Use **Cython, PyPy, or Rust bindings** for performance-heavy tasks |
| Memory Usage | Optimize with **Numba, generators, and** `slots` |
| Database Scaling | Use **PostgreSQL, DynamoDB, or Firebase for cloud databases** |
| Concurrency | Use **asyncio for non-blocking I/O operations** |
| Serverless Scaling | Deploy with **AWS Lambda, Google Cloud Functions** |

**Best Practice: Use a combination of profiling tools** (`cProfile`, `Py-Spy`, `memory_profiler`) to identify bottlenecks and optimize performance.

# 3.2 Automating Deployment and Continuous Integration (CI/CD)

To ensure **cross-platform compatibility and seamless updates**, applications should use **automated deployment pipelines**.

*Using GitHub Actions for CI/CD Deployment*

```yaml
name: Deploy App
on:
  push:
    branches:
      - main

jobs:
  build:
    runs-on: ubuntu-latest
    steps:
      - uses: actions/checkout@v2
      - name: Set up Python
        uses: actions/setup-python@v2
        with:
          python-version: "3.9"
      - name: Install Dependencies
        run: pip install -r requirements.txt
      - name: Run Tests
        run: pytest
```

**Best Practice: Automate testing and deployment to ensure stability across different platforms**.

# *3.3 Cloud Deployment and Containerization*

Cloud-based deployment ensures **scalability and flexibility**.

| Deployment Strategy | Best Practice |
|---|---|
| Containerization | Use **Docker** to package applications for portability |
| Orchestration | Use **Kubernetes** for large-scale deployments |
| Serverless | Deploy with **AWS Lambda, Firebase Functions** |
| Cloud Hosting | Use **AWS, Google Cloud, Azure** |

*Example: Dockerizing a Python API*
dockerfile

```
FROM python:3.9

WORKDIR /app
COPY . /app
RUN pip install -r requirements.txt

CMD ["python", "app.py"]
```

**Best Practice: Use containers to make applications portable across multiple platforms**.

---

# Conclusion

Long-term success in **cross-platform Python development** requires:

1. **Selecting the right frameworks and databases** for scalability.

2. **Keeping up with emerging trends** like **serverless, WebAssembly, and AI integration**.
3. **Optimizing and automating deployments** to scale applications effectively.

## *Key Takeaways:*

- **Choose the right technology stack** for each platform.
- **Engage with the open-source community** to stay ahead of trends.
- **Automate testing and deployments** for scalability.
- **Optimize performance** using **Cython, Rust, or PyPy**.
- **Deploy applications via containers and serverless platforms**.

# The End of This Book, but the Beginning of Your Journey

This book has provided a **comprehensive guide to cross-platform Python development**, from **building and deploying applications** to **scaling and securing them**.

Your journey doesn't stop here! **Continue experimenting, learning, and building!**

◆ **Next Steps:**
Start a new project using **modern cross-platform frameworks**.
Contribute to **open-source Python projects**.
Explore **AI, WebAssembly, and serverless deployment**.
Stay updated with **emerging Python technologies**.

**Have questions or want additional resources?** Let me know, and I'll provide recommendations to help you master cross-platform Python development!

www.ingramcontent.com/pod-product-compliance
Lightning Source LLC
LaVergne TN
LVHW051438050326
832903LV00030BD/3150